The Complete Guide to Running Successful

Workshops & Seminars

*Everything You Need to Know
to Plan, Promote, and Present a
Conference Explained Simply*

BY KRISTIE LORETTE

The Complete Guide to Running Successful Workshops & Seminars: Everything You Need to Know to Plan, Promote, and Present a Conference Explained Simply

Copyright © 2014 by Atlantic Publishing Group, Inc.
1405 SW 6th Ave. • Ocala, Florida 34471 • 800-814-1132 • 352-622-1875–Fax
Website: www.atlantic-pub.com • Email: sales@atlantic-pub.com
SAN Number: 268-1250

Library of Congress Cataloging-in-Publication Data

Lorette, Kristie, 1975-
The complete guide to running successful workshops & seminars : everything you need to know to plan, promote, and present a conference explained simply / by Kristie Lorette.
p. cm.
Includes bibliographical references and index.
ISBN 978-1-60138-613-7 (alk. paper) -- ISBN 1-60138-613-3
1. Seminars--Planning. 2. Workshops (Adult education)--Planning. 3. Congresses and conventions--Planning. 4. Continuing education--Planning. I. Title. II. Title: Complete guide to running successful workshops and seminars.
LC6519.L67 2012
808.53--dc23
2012030111

Printed in the United States
BOOK PRODUCTION DESIGN: T.L. Price • design@tlpricefreelance.com

A few years back we lost our beloved pet dog Bear, who was not only our best and dearest friend but also the "Vice President of Sunshine" here at Atlantic Publishing. He did not receive a salary but worked tirelessly 24 hours a day to please his parents.

Bear was a rescue dog who turned around and showered myself, my wife, Sherri, his grandparents Jean, Bob, and Nancy, and every person and animal he met (well, maybe not rabbits) with friendship and love. He made a lot of people smile every day.

We wanted you to know a portion of the profits of this book will be donated in Bear's memory to local animal shelters, parks, conservation organizations, and other individuals and nonprofit organizations in need of assistance.

— Douglas & Sherri Brown

PS: We have since adopted two more rescue dogs: first Scout, and the following year, Ginger. They were both mixed golden retrievers who needed a home.

Want to help animals and the world? Here are a dozen easy suggestions you and your family can implement today:

- *Adopt and rescue a pet from a local shelter.*
- *Support local and no-kill animal shelters.*
- *Plant a tree to honor someone you love.*
- *Be a developer — put up some birdhouses.*
- *Buy live, potted Christmas trees and replant them.*
- *Make sure you spend time with your animals each day.*
- *Save natural resources by recycling and buying recycled products.*
- *Drink tap water, or filter your own water at home.*
- *Whenever possible, limit your use of or do not use pesticides.*
- *If you eat seafood, make sustainable choices.*
- *Support your local farmers market.*
- *Get outside. Visit a park, volunteer, walk your dog, or ride your bike.*

Five years ago, Atlantic Publishing signed the Green Press Initiative. These guidelines promote environmentally friendly practices, such as using recycled stock and vegetable-based inks, avoiding waste, choosing energy-efficient resources, and promoting a no-pulping policy. We now use 100-percent recycled stock on all our books. The results: in one year, switching to post-consumer recycled stock saved 24 mature trees, 5,000 gallons of water, the equivalent of the total energy used for one home in a year, and the equivalent of the greenhouse gases from one car driven for a year.

Table of Contents

Chapter 2: Logistics: Date, Time, Place 47

Chapter 3: Creating a Budget 63

Chapter 4: Establishing Your Team of Professionals................................ 79

Chapter 5: Funding, Sponsors, and Donations 95

Chapter 6: Get Ready to Deliver 105

Table of Contents

Chapter 7: Marketing the Seminar & Workshop to the Right Audience 127

Chapter 8: Deliver 161

Chapter 9: Working with Attendees 175

Chapter 10: Mistakes and Disasters and How to Avoid Them 183

Chapter 11: Evaluating the Seminar and Workshop Success 191

Chapter 12: What You Need to Do if You Are Setting up an Event, Workshop, Seminar, or Conference Planning Business 201

Table of Contents

Introduction

As you read this book, workshops and seminars are unfolding around the world. Traditionally, workshops and seminars are educational environments to which employers send their employees so they can learn about the industry in which they work. In  modern times, however, seminars and workshops have become a popular way for companies, experts, and associations to share information on the latest trends in an industry and to provide valuable tips and advice on a number of topics.

If you are reading this, you likely are thinking about hosting your own seminars or workshops for your business. Or you might be reading this guide because you have been put in charge of planning and running a seminar or workshop for your company, association, or other membership group. No matter how you came to be planning a workshop or seminar, make sure said event is the best. Rather than having potential employees roll their eyes when they find out they have to attend, you want them to be excited about attending.

The Complete Guide to Running Successful Workshops & Seminars is your stepping-stone to planning and pulling off an effective conference that is sure to be a hit from start to finish. Each chapter of the book walks you through the multitude of steps you have to take to plan a seminar or workshop. What makes this guide different is that it provides you with tips and advice to make your conference stand out from the rest in your industry. You also will find checklists, worksheets, and more that you can use in the planning process.

Along with the logistics of planning a workshop and seminar, filling the seats with the right audience members is the key to a successful event. This guide has it covered. You will discover online and offline marketing techniques that attract the attendees who will most benefit from the information sharing sessions. You will learn who these audience members are, the way your marketing materials will speak to them, and how to motivate them to sign up for your event.

Even after the event is over, your work as the planner is not finished. The guide reveals what you need to do to evaluate the success of your event. It also helps you use this information to plan future events to increase the success rates of these events or to reach your other goals in hosting seminars and workshops.

How to Use this Book

The first time you crack this guide open, read it from beginning to end. You do not have to do this in one sitting, but the first time you read it, avoid taking action because so much information is packed in that you need to take the time to absorb it before you jump in and start using the information right away. Reading the guide completely allows you to obtain a big picture view of the task you have ahead of you. Once you have the big picture view, you have all the information you need to start tackling the steps.

After you finish going through the book, you should have the blueprint for your workshop or seminar. The guide also makes a good reference resource. Even after planning workshops and seminars multiple times, you will find that returning to the guide refreshes your mind. After gaining some experience hosting these events, you also start to see the information in the guide in a different light. You can make more effective use of the information once you have a workshop or seminar or two under your belt.

Who Might Organize a Workshop or Seminar?

When you think of workshops and seminars, what probably pops into your mind is an employer asking his or her employees to attend an industry conference. The company ships its employees off to a far-off city for multiple days of boring lectures and a stroll on the conference room floor,  where the employees can network and pick up information on other companies that serve their industry. Although these types of conferences do take place, today more businesses, companies, experts, and associations are using seminars and workshops for other purposes. If you are not sure if a seminar or workshop is right for your situation, consider some of the professionals using this format to promote and market their business, industry, and more.

Some of the people, groups, and professionals who might organize a workshop or seminar include:

- **Business owner** — A business owner has the opportunity to use a workshop or seminar as an indirect or soft-sell method for promoting his or her goods and services. Any type of business can benefit from effectively planned seminars and workshops. For example, a marketing professional might host a small business seminar that teaches small business owners a seven-step approach to creating effective marketing pieces. The marketing professional is using the seminar/workshop format to convince the attendees that they need him or her to create these marketing pieces for them while sharing advice and information on the topic. Some of the audience members will indeed take the information the marketing professional provides and apply it to their own work. Others, however, will end up hiring the marketing professional if he or she does a good job of building credibility and expertise on the topic.

- **Sales professional** — Professionals employed by companies also use this format to make sales. Seminars and workshops fill a room with potential customers and help sales professionals build a lead list of potential customers for the future. A good example of sales professionals who use workshops and seminars are real estate and mortgage professionals. A mortgage professional might team up with a real estate professional to host a seminar for first-time home buyers. Professionals share information on how a first-time home buyer should find and finance a home in the current housing market. The goal is to paint the person as the expert whom the attendees would want to work with when buying and financing their first home, but in a soft approach. This does not mean cramming the sales pitch down their throats.

- **Industry expert** — If you are an expert in your field, you can use seminars and workshops to sell your services or products. Again, you are sharing just enough of your expertise on a topic to convince attendees they want to buy the services or products you are selling. A wedding industry expert is one example. As a professional wedding planner, you might host a seminar on the seven biggest mistakes first-time brides make when planning their weddings. Share some information on each mistake and how to avoid it. By the end of the seminar, some of the brides will realize they need a professional like you to handle their weddings so they can avoid making all the mistakes.

- **Membership organization** — Membership organizations are another group that can benefit from hosting workshops and seminars. Educational workshops and seminars are part of the member benefits package you promote to bring in new members of your association. They create a win-win situation in many circumstances because the members obtain information and networking opportunities that they need, and the membership organization might make some money by selling admission to the events that can be used to create additional benefits for the members. For example, wedding vendors who are members of the National Association of Wedding Professionals attend an annual meeting. The meeting has several different components, but most of the event includes seminars and workshops in which the vendors learn how to market their wedding business. Seminars and workshops have topics that cover the latest trends in the industry that pertain to the members, but the event also has an annual awards dinner, along with social and networking opportunities.

- **Industry organization** — Some organizations cater directly to an industry. These industries can range from scientists and pharmaceuticals to wedding planners and other companies that cater to the wedding industry. These types of workshops and seminars are two-fold. First, it is an information-sharing session in which attendees can pick up information on industry news, trends, advice, and tips. Second, it is a networking opportunity for members of the industry to meet one another and possibly to do business with in the future. At many industry conferences, the hosts try to sell products or services, or they allow attending companies or vendors to attend the show to sell products or services. For example, business professionals in the eco-friendly building industry might attend a seminar or workshop to learn about the latest trends, regulations, and laws for building environmentally friendly residential and commercial properties.

What Types of Workshops and Seminars Exist?

When you think of seminars and workshops, different types of events can fall under these categories. Although Chapter 1 of this guide provides a more thorough definition of what seminars and workshops are, seven primary types of workshops and seminars exist. Here is a brief overview of them:

1. **Keynote speaker event** — A motivational event that lasts a few hours

2. **Teaching event** — An environment in which one or more speakers is teaching the audience on topics related to the industry or audience in attendance

3. **Hands-on learning workshop** — The attendees participate in activities to learn the information.

4. **Learning and networking event** — Combination event in which speakers share information to teach audience members. Social events or

breakout times allow the attendees to network with one another and with the industry professionals speaking at the sessions.

5. **Learning, networking, and sales event** — Combination event that contains all the features of a learning and networking event. The hosts or speakers at the event also make their products or services available for attendees to buy.

6. **Learning, hands-on learning, and networking** — Combination event in which speakers teach the audience members, audience members attend breakout sessions for hands-on learning opportunities, and social events allow for networking among attendees.

7. **Learning, hands-on learning, networking, and sales** — Combination event in which speakers teach the audience members, audience members attend breakout sessions for hands-on learning opportunities, and social events allow for networking among attendees. Additionally, the hosts or speakers at the event make their products or services available for purchase.

With a better understanding of the various formats of seminars and workshops, it is time to get into the details of what a seminar and workshop entail, what you need to do to put together sizzling events that attract the right audience, and how to reach your goals for hosting the events.

Chapter One

What are Workshops and Seminars?

In the first chapter of the book, you will find a more detailed explanation of what seminars and workshops are. You will obtain more details on what these events look like and what kinds of information or topics are covered. Additionally, the chapter helps you walk through the steps of setting a purpose for your seminar or workshop: Is it to sell services or products you offer, to make money conducting seminars and workshops, or to provide a learning environment for a particular topic or industry?

You also will uncover information on how to choose the primary topic and subtopics for the seminar or workshop — topics that will attract the right audience and make you money. Last, you will discover how long the workshop or seminar should be, how and where attendees should check in, and the seating arrangements. Set up a preliminary plan on this information up front, so you can plan the logistics of the event, such as setting the date, time, and potential locations.

Workshops and Seminars Defined

In the introduction, you learned about the seven primary types of seminars and workshops. Now, it is time for you to learn about each type of event in more detail so that you can determine the format of your event — the format

conducive to the learning and delivery that best fits your audience members and the hosts of the event.

According to Webster's Dictionary, a seminar is a small group of students, as in a university, that meets regularly to exchange information, hold discussions, and engage in advanced study and original research under a member of the faculty.

The same dictionary defines workshops as a seminar, discussion group, or the like that emphasizes exchange of ideas and the demonstration and application of techniques and skills.

The primary difference between a seminar and a workshop is that a seminar provides more of a one-way exchange of information and ideas, while a workshop establishes a two-way street of communication. The hosts of these events have taken this information a step further and created seven different formats for planning seminars and workshops for a particular audience:

1. **Keynote speaker event** — One of the primary formats for a seminar is a keynote speaker event. The keynote speaker gives a motivational speech that lasts from one to two hours. Keynote speaker events can be for any audience, such as mortgage sales professionals or scientists. Because the nature of keynote speaking is motivational, the speaker is telling a story or sharing information with the group in an effort to compel them to be better sales people, scientists, students, or whatever attendees make

up the audience. Depending on the popularity of the speaker, he or she might give the same speech multiple times to reach all the attendees.

2. **Teaching event** — A teaching event has more of a classroom feel to it, where one or more rooms are set up for speakers or lecturers to take the stage. Each speaker has a industry- or audience-related topic, with an ultimate goal of sharing educational information, tips, advice, industry news, or trends that relate to the theme of the event. Many speakers provide packets of information, workbooks, or handouts to help attendees implement the information. The setup for a teaching event is similar to that of a keynote speaker event.

3. **Hands-on learning event** — You start to seep over into a workshop event with hands-on learning opportunities. In workshops, the attendees participate in activities to learn the information the speaker is sharing. Workshops contain smaller audiences than keynote speaker events and teaching events. Although these other events might contain hundreds of people, workshops tend to remain as small as five and up to about 20 people. The sessions remain small so each attendee has the opportunity to learn and then implement what he or she has learned by performing an activity under the supervision of the teacher. Attendees learn from the teacher of the workshop and learn from their peers and colleagues. The setup for workshops requires multiple rooms, so different workshops can occur at the same time. Each workshop has multiple time slots so attendees can move between rooms for their assigned time slot.

4. **Learning and networking event** — Most events are a combination of activities that combine the characteristics of a seminar with those of a workshop. At a learning and networking event, speakers share information to teach audience members. Social events or breakout times allow the attendees to network with each other and with the industry professionals that are speaking. The sessions for these types of events might be a larger

group for the primary speaker and networking sessions but remain small for the activities so that each attendee has the opportunity to learn with some direction from the moderator. These types of events allow attendees to learn from the teacher and their colleagues. The setup for workshops requires multiple rooms for different workshops occurring at the same time. Each workshop has multiple time slots so attendees can move between rooms for their assigned time slot.

5. **Learning, networking, and sales event** — Another combination event provides sessions in which speakers share information to teach audience members. Social events or breakout times allow the attendees to network with each other and with the industry professionals. Additionally, the hosts or speakers at the event make their products or services available. These types of events tend to be larger than the previously mentioned events. They also require more space as far as setup is concerned. The learning and networking setup tends to be similar to learning and networking environments. The difference is that they have a trade show floor component in which vendors participating in the event set up tables and displays to sell their products or services.

6. **Learning, hands-on learning, and networking** — This is a combination event in which speakers teach the audience members, audience members attend breakout sessions for hands-on learning opportunities, and social events allow for networking among attendees. These events require multiple rooms to host the different learning environments and create the hands-on learning classrooms. Although networking takes place as a part of the other two aspects of the event, these events have one or more social functions where all the attendees are in the same room for networking purposes.

7. **Learning, hands-on learning, networking, and sales** — A combination event in which speakers teach the audience members, audience members

attend breakout sessions for hands-on learning opportunities, and social events allow for networking among attendees. Additionally, the hosts or speakers at the event make their products or services available. This is the biggest and most complex type of event to organize because it has many different components. The event tends to draw the largest number of attendees, so you will need the most space and a larger amount of rooms than the other events. Because these are the most comprehensive types of events, they also can be the most productive.

Set a Purpose

Seminars, workshops, conferences, and trade shows all have different purposes. Some professionals host these events as an indirect way to sell services or products. Other hosts want to make money off the admission tickets. The majority of these events combine several purposes. When it comes to nonprofit organizations, associations, and membership groups, most of the events provide a learning environment on a topic that relates to the attendees and the organization. The final purpose is to provide a networking opportunity for attendees to interact with, refer business to, or do business with one another.

Before you can get into the planning process, first determine what your purpose is for hosting your event. If you are not sure, read on to find more details on the various purposes. Each purpose also includes an example so you then can correlate it to your own event.

Sell services

One reason to host seminars and workshops is to use the event as a way to gather leads for prospects. If you design the topic or topics to attract your ideal clients, you know you have a room full of potential buyers. Using seminars and workshops to sell services is an indirect sales method because you are not bringing them into the room to run a hard-core sales session, but instead, you are showing them how they could benefit from your services and letting them figure the rest out for themselves.

Use an educational or informational format. With this format, you share your expertise and knowledge to build credibility with the audience members. Your goal is to create a situation in which the audience members see you as such an expert that they hire you on  the spot. You at least want them to think of you in the future when they need one of the services you provide.

Ideally, you are gathering contact information from attendees before the event and at the check-in. This allows you to build your lead list and database of prospects with whom you can continue to communicate in an attempt to convert them into paying clients at some point down the road.

Numerous types of service-based businesses use this approach for indirectly selling their services. One example is an accounting expert. Assume her target audience is small business owners and entrepreneurs. She might hold a conference on the tax benefits of running a small business, specifically geared toward the needs and wants of small business owners and entrepreneurs. The title of the event might be, "Five Ways Small Business Owners Can Save the Money They Owe to Uncle Sam."

The accounting professional sets an agenda for the event that starts with a brief introduction of what she does and how she helps small business owners and entrepreneurs manage their finances for tax purposes. Then, she moves on and covers the top five ways small business owners and entrepreneurs should handle their finances to save money on their taxes. Last, the accounting professional covers the ways she helps small businesses to set up accounting systems and procedures to maximize their tax savings and make it simpler to file taxes during tax season, which is promoting her own services. At the end of the event, she offers attendees a free, 30-minute consultation to work on a review of the current accounting system the business is using.

The idea is that the accounting professional uses the 30-minute session to up-sell the business owner on her services. Some attendees will ask her about any additional services she provides, and some will even hire her on the spot. Others will contact her later. The accounting professional will continue to communicate with these attendees in an attempt to continue to convert any remaining prospects into clients.

In this case, the purpose of the event is to sell services. The accounting professional is using the event as the format to showcase her expertise. By building a relationship with attendees, she has a higher chance of converting attendees into paying clients.

Sell products

A similar purpose for hosting a seminar or workshop event is to sell tangible products. Everything that pertains to selling services also pertains to selling products. The only real difference is that the attendees can walk away with one or more of the products in their hands.

For example, a real estate attorney might sell a DIY kit on how to apply for a loan modification with lenders for consumers to buy. A commercial cleaning company might host a seminar on the best ways to keep the germs at bay and your employees at their desk during flu season while selling commercial-grade cleaning products at the back of the room.

Make money

Some hosts of seminars and workshops schedule the events for the specific purpose of making money. In other words, the seats or admissions are how they make a profit. In many circumstances, these events are educational in nature. In this case, the event hosts are selling tickets for the attendees to walk away with educational materials, fresh ideas, tips, and advice. In return, the event hosts walk away

with money in their pockets, even after covering the costs for throwing the event.

A for-profit business that puts on seminars and workshops pockets this money. If a nonprofit organization hosts a similar event, the money it makes is considered a donation to the organization. The donation money then is used to promote and fulfill the purpose of the organization.

As an example, a pharmacists association might host an educational forum, in which pharmacists can come and learn various things about running a successful pharmacy. The association uses the admission money to cover the costs of the event. Additionally, the profit the association earns goes toward paying for awards and trophies for the annual award ceremony.

Provide learning environment

Another purpose for these types of events is educational or informational. The price for admission covers the costs the hosts incur for throwing the event. In other circumstances, the events are free to attendees, so the costs come out of the host's pocket instead. The host has a budget set for these events, which are funded by another source, such as sponsors or membership fees.

For example, a research university might host an annual convention for scientists. Each workshop or seminar breakout session might include industry news, breaks in research on specific topics, and presentations of new instruments and machines scientists are using in experiments.

Networking opportunities

A purpose of almost all types of seminars and workshops is networking. Attendees have the opportunity to network with the experts and vendors at the event. In some circumstances, attendees might even be able to network with one another. Some hosts build social events into the agenda, which spark conversations between attendees. Other events have vendors on the trade show floor to hand out information on their companies, products, and services and to start conversations with potential buyers and referral sources. Small group activities, such as breakout sessions, also foster networking among the attendees of that particular session.

A good example of this is an alternative energy source association composed of members that sell products and services related to alternative energy sources. During certain hours of the day or days of the event, company attendees have a table, and their displays are set up on the trade show floor. Attendees can wander between tables to collect information and talk with the business representatives.

Combination

The most common purpose of a seminar is a combination of the purposes listed here in this chapter. Workshops and seminars commonly have different elements on the agenda, so you might find educational workshops taking place in one area of the event while another area introduces products and services attendees find useful.

CASE STUDY: REACHING THE APEX: SETTING & MEASURING GOALS FOR SEMINARS

Apex Power Publishing
Lia Tutt, ACB
3709 Alabama Avenue SE
Suite #302
Washington, DC 20020
(443) 540-3721
www.apexpowerpublishing.com

Apex Power Publishing is a consulting business offering customized manuals to help its clients achieve their goals and dreams. Lia Tutt from Apex Power Publishing shares that consulting is an experience, so clients see the value of Apex Power Consulting Services better when they experience a sample of the services in the form of a seminar or a workshop. This format permits the individuals and business professionals that are attending to see how the Apex Power Publishing services add value to their own business. Because services are not tangible, workshops and seminars create an environment where attendees can experience firsthand the benefit of the customized manuals the publisher producers.

When Tutt hosts a seminar or workshop, the primary goal is to sign more clients to use the manuals the company produces and to use Apex Power Publishing's consulting services. The workshops Tutt hosts are educational in nature, so she is able to position herself as an expert. Tutt also works with a partner, which is another company or organization, on hosting the event. This allows Tutt to presell her products and programs that include a markup for the partnering company or organization to make money from the sales as well.

For example, one of Tutt's packages is $50 per person, which includes the workbook and four weeks of group consulting services. The partnering business receives $30 per person. If 60 people attend this particular seminar, then the partnering company makes $1,800 and Tutt receives the other $1,200. For her deluxe programs at $2,000 each, the partnering company receives 40 percent of the sales, and Tutt keeps the other 60 percent. If Tutt signs ten deluxe program clients, who receive weekly consulting sessions for six months, the total amount that comes in the door is $20,000, with 40 percent going to the partner company and 60 percent to Tutt.

Tutt measures the success of each of her events by setting a specific goal for each event. Her goal is for 30 percent of the attendees to be prospective clients for her business and to convert 10 percent of attendees into new clients now. Her goal is for the remaining 20 percent of the prospective clients to do business with her at some point in the future as their schedule permits.

Tutt also suggests that hosts have attendees complete a survey that can help guide you on the ways they are looking for you to help them. Include questions on future topic suggestion as well. Include a section where they can list the strengths of the event and where there is some room for improvement. Finally, you want to gather contact information so that you can contact them after the seminar to schedule a meeting, and to add their information to your database for future marketing and communication.

Identifying the Ideal Audience

Now that you have set a purpose for your seminars and workshops, it is time to get to know the people who will make up the audience at your event. To plan and implement the seminars and workshops, you first have to know whom to attract with your marketing materials and who will be sitting in the seats as the event unfolds. How can you put together a website or a marketing brochure to attract readers if you do not know their needs and wants? The same holds true when it is time to book speakers, plan activities, and put together the presentation materials.

For example, if your audience were a group of biophysicists, the language, terminology, and approach you use would be quite different from an audience of small business owners or marketing professionals. You might want to narrow it down even more, such as attracting small business owners of catering companies.

You want to specifically mention your target audience in your marketing materials. Many conferences, workshops, and seminars state exactly who should consider attending the event. You will find a list in the marketing materials that says, "The professionals and businesses that should attend are:

- Small business owners
- Entrepreneurs
- Freelancers
- Marketing directors
- Marketing vice presidents
- Marketing regional directors
- Marketing associates

When identifying your ideal audience, be as specific and detailed as possible. This helps you position your marketing materials to attract the right people and sets the stage for putting together the presentation and information materials. *Chapter 7 covers the details of creating effective and efficient marketing materials to promote your event and attract attendees.*

When you are deciding who will benefit the most from the information, products, and services at your event, think about details, such as:

- Where do your participants live?
- Where do they work?

- What do they like to do in their spare time?

- In what industries do they work?

- What is the average household income?

- Business income?

- What is the average education level?

- What are their needs and wants?

- Which individuals or groups most benefit from the information you intend to share?

- If applicable, which gender will most likely benefit from the information?

- Age range?

This information provides you with a starting point from which to work. Some marketing experts suggest writing a profile of your ideal audience member, even giving him or her a name, background, age, profession, and other personal and professional information. The more details you can provide, the better equipped you will be to put together the most effective marketing and information materials possible.

For example, a welfare organization is hosting a "How to Babysit" workshop. The profile of its ideal attendee might read like this:

Sally Smith is a 25- to 36-year-old woman. She lives in the metro Detroit area of Michigan. She is married and has zero to two children of her own. She works at home and runs an in-home day care business. Her spouse works out of the home five days a week. Sally is looking for a workshop that will help her learn the foundational aspects of starting and running a safe day care out of her home.

Sally's husband makes $50,000 in gross income per year. Sally is looking to bring in about $25,000 per year in gross income from her at-home day care. Sally has a high school education and earned her college degree in early childhood development. She started working in a day care and as a preschool teacher, which she did for three years before having her own children. Sally is looking to earn some additional money for her household while also having the chance to put her education and experience to work.

Once you have a profile created, you are ready to consider the workshop, seminar topics, and subtopics that are most likely to appeal to the audience.

Market Area Research

"Market" is one way of referring to a city or a metropolitan statistical area (MSA). MSA is a term used in census research. Decide on a target city for your event, workshop, or seminar. Start looking at various parts of the city. Focus on the parts that would be good for your particular type of event.

Trade area research — Trade area refers to the area from which most of your customers will come.

Site research — After you have narrowed down your choices, it is time to look at the sites. Take pictures, make notes, and evaluate the various sites to determine which is best for your event.

You can use the following list to evaluate a potential event site:

- Downtown area
- Historic district
- Business district
- Government offices
- Colleges/universities
- Technical schools
- Religious schools
- Military bases
- Hospitals
- Major highway

- Beaches/ocean
- Mountains
- Lakes
- Nature preserves
- State parks
- Zoos
- Sports arenas
- Hotels
- Rivers
- Shopping

Evaluate these specifics about any location you are considering:

- How many similar events, workshops, or seminars take place in the area?
- Find sales volume for the type of event you are hosting.
- Are there colleges or student housing in the area?
- Are there a high number of working mothers in the area?
- What is the population of the immediate area?
- Is the population increasing, stationary, or declining?
- Are the residents of all ages or old, middle-aged, or young?
- What is the average sales price and rental rates for area homes?
- What is the per capita income?
- Find the average family size.
- Is the location suitable for the type of event, workshop, seminar, or conference you are hosting?

Population and Demographics

Population and demographics are factors to consider when choosing a location for your event as well. Places to obtain the details you need include the U.S. Census Bureau, **www.census.gov**, which can supply important information and statistics about the event, workshop, seminar, and conference industry.

Demographics to evaluate include:

- Population density
- Personal income
- Age groups
- Ethnic populations
- Employment statistics

Another good source for information is the local chamber of commerce. To contact a chamber in another area, go to **www.chamberofcommerce.com**. You can get in touch with the association related to the industry your event focuses on, and peers will assist you with economic and lifestyle patterns for your business research.

Your library and online sources can provide valuable information. Research librarians can help you. A website you should check out is DemographicsNow®, at **www.demographicsnow.com**. Find out the market statistics in different areas of the United States.

Industry Information

For additional data and statistics, visit the following sites online:

- QuickFacts: **http://quickfacts.census.gov/qfd/index.html**

- SearchBug®: **www.searchbug.com/sitemap.aspx**

- MelissaData®: **www.melissadata.com/lookups/index.htm**

The American Community Survey: **www.census.gov/acs** — Provides additional information from the supplemental census survey. This information includes demographics by county and metropolitan statistical areas (MSAs). An MSA is an area with at least one major city and includes the county or counties located within the MSA. This survey is replacing the Census Bureau's long survey. It provides full demographic information for communities each year, not every ten years.

CenStats Databases: **http://censtats.census.gov** — This website provides economic and demographic information that you can compare by county. The information is updated every two years.

County Business Patterns: **www.census.gov/econ/cbp/index.html** — Economic information is reported by industry, and the statistics are updated each year. Statistics include the number of establishments, employment, and payroll for more than 40,000 ZIP codes across the country. Metro Business Patterns provides the same data for MSAs.

American FactFinder: **http://factfinder.census.gov** — Allows you to evaluate all sorts of U.S. census data

Scouting the Competition

Never underestimate the value of knowing your competition. Make a list of the other events, workshops, seminars, and conferences in your market. Which ones target the same population that you will? Find out what they are offering and selling at their events, and the prices they are charging for admission and more.

Take a detailed look at your competition when you narrow down your choices. The information you want can be hard to find. The best way to find information about your competition may be a visit to their events. Be creative.

Other sources of information on competition include the following ideas:

- Telephone book — Will give you the number and location of your competitors.

- Chambers of Commerce — They have lists of local businesses. Verify whether it is a complete list, not just Chamber members.

- Local newspapers — Study the local advertisements and help wanted ads. There also could be a weekly entertainment section with information about local events, workshops, seminars, and conferences taking place in the area.

Mark your proposed location on a street map. You can determine how far to research, depending on how far you believe people will travel for your event.

Once you determine your target area, visit every event that is similar to the type of event you are hosting.

- What did and did not work for you while you were attending the event?

- Do the other attendees seem to like the surroundings and the event offerings?

- How busy is the event at peak times?

- Do they offer anything unique?

- How many attendees can they serve at a time?
- What is the atmosphere?
- When are the busy periods?

How to Choose Workshop and Seminar Topics that Sizzle

With a clear picture of who is occupying the seats at your event, you are ready to assemble the sizzling topics they are there to hear. If you work in the industry the event covers, you have firsthand experience in what audience members are interested in learning more about. Whether you fit the profile of your potential audience members or not, you have to uncover topics that are interesting and relevant to the people who are there. Fortunately, you have numerous sources to turn to for gathering ideas, creating your own ideas, and developing content for your event.

One area to glean ideas from is to look at the trends for the industry or area the conference covers. For example, if it is an event for manufacturing professionals, you might consider covering a production trend, such as innovative ways the manufacturing professionals can use joint venture partners and affiliates to increase sales.

Peruse some industry and mainstream publications for articles, tips, tricks, advice, and information that relate to the seminars and workshops you will be hosting. Although you might not want to copy the topic verbatim, it is certainly a foundation from which you can build your own topic. You might even be able to use the articles or information to put your own twist on the topic. For example, an article of the latest accounting software programs could be tailored as a topic for medium-sized business finance professionals managing the accounting setup and management for the business.

The reasons these publications are good sources of information are two-fold. First, if an article is in the publication, it is a topic readers are interested in learning more about. Second, it is important to research the author, writer, or journalist of an interesting topic. When the authors are experts in their field, they might be potential speakers and teachers for your seminars. Although you have not reached the point of being ready to start booking speakers and mediators, you can take note of these experts during the research process.

Pick up local, regional, and national publications. Although a local publication might be right for the immediate area, you might need to expand or modify the topics to attract audience members from other areas.

Surveys are another good source of information. You can create your own survey and send it out to the audience members you are trying to attract. Have them complete and return the survey to guide you in the types of seminars and workshops they are most interested in attending. If you have an event planned, survey the current audience to find out what relevant and juicy topics they would want to come back to for the next time you have an event. This option requires that you have an audience or mailing list of the ideal attendees on hand.

If this is not your situation, fret not, because surveys are still a viable option. Search online, at the local library, and in publications for survey results. Big firms, marketing research companies, and other organizations sponsor surveys and focus groups to gather information on a subject or relevant topic. They often publish these survey results for others to read. You can garner a multitude of facts from these surveys and turn them into creative topics that sell the seats to your event.

For example, an investment firm conducts an annual survey to find out how parents are saving for the college education of their children. The survey results reveal that more parents are saving more money than they did in previous years, and they are looking for savings accounts that provide tax advantages to them and their children when they use the money in the account.

If you are an investment adviser or estate planner, this is a treasure trove of information for you to put together a seminar regarding the types of college savings plans parents can use, how much they need to save, and when they need to start saving.

Online websites that publish press releases are another good find for coming up with popular topics. When you conduct your online searches, you might find press releases posted on business websites, blogs, or other types of websites. Press release sites also exist; you can go right to the source and search under categories that pertain to the type of workshop or seminar you are looking to host. A few sites to consider include:

- **www.clickpress.com**
- **http://prweb.com**
- **www.prnewswire.com**
- **www.webwire.com**
- **http://pressexposure.com**
- **www.przoom.com**
- **www.addpr.com/addrelease.php**
- **www.directionsmag.com/pressreleases/add**
- **www.free-press-release.com**

Save this list for later because you can also use these sites when it comes time to market and promote your own event. *Chapter 7 covers the marketing and promotion of your event.*

Your direct and indirect competition is another way to generate ideas that you know will sell or be popular with the crowd. Search for conferences, trade shows, seminars, and workshops on your topic. Review the agendas to evaluate the topics and formats. Look at similar workshop and seminar topics. You also might be able to update or put a new twist on an old topic.

Another aspect to consider is the availability of speakers and experts to cover the topics. You might not need the specific name of the person you want to land, but be aware of whether experts or speakers exist to cover the topics. If not, think about whether you are able to cover a certain topic yourself or are able to acquire someone who can handle running the session.

Seminar and Workshop Formats

You also will have to choose formats for delivering the topics. The types of formats are up to you, the speakers, educators, and what you think the best teaching and learning format is for the information being shared.

Some of the formats to consider:

- **Standard classroom style** — You can go different ways with this format. You can have chairs in the audience or tables set up to resemble a standard classroom. The advantage of this setup is that it is quick and easy. Plus, it allows attendees a place for sitting and taking notes. The disadvantage is that this is a one-level setup, which means the speaker and attendees are all on the same level. For large room events, it can be difficult for attendees in the back of the room to hear and see the speaker.

- **Speaker on stage/platform with chairs/tables on the floor** — This setup has similar advantages to the standard classroom-style setup. The primary advantage is that the speaker is on a level above the audience, which makes it easier for everyone in the room to hear and see the speaker, no matter where he or she is sitting. The primary disadvantage is that this requires more money for renting a platform or stage for the speaker.

- **Interactive workshop stations/tables** — These types of setups are used in smaller rooms for breakout sessions. The primary advantage is that this setup breaks big groups of attendees into smaller groups. The primary disadvantage is the need and cost for multiple rooms at the event.

- **Discussion/brainstorming sessions** — This setup also requires multiple small rooms for the different sessions. Multiple rooms equal an increased rental rate and the need for a venue that offers such amenities.

- **Q&A sessions** — When it is one large Q&A session, your venue only requires chairs for the audience and a place for the speaker to stand. For larger sessions, you might need a stage or platform and even audiovisual equipment. You might need a microphone for the speaker and an additional one for the attendees who are asking questions, depending on the size of the group. This is the least formal type of event, in that a discussion is not planned, but rather the speaker is soliciting questions from the audience.

Depending on your topics and purpose for holding the event, you could have any and all these formats present at your convention. Some of the most successful conferences incorporate all these formats at different times to accomplish different tasks.

The formats you choose will guide you through assessing the types and number of rooms you need for your event. The formats also help you set a preliminary agenda for the event.

With some ideas on the format of the seminar and workshop, now it is time to start planning the dates, times, and locations of your events. *In Chapter 2, you will learn how to plan these aspects of the event.*

Chapter Two
Logistics: Date, Time, Place

Timing is everything, so you will want to choose the best date, time, and place to host your seminars and workshops. In Chapter 2, you will learn how to identify dates and times that are sure to be convenient for you and your potential attendees. You also do not want your seminar or workshop to be competing with another event that might steal your audience away. After settling on some potential dates  and times, you also will learn what to look for in a venue. Choosing a venue — the right location — is a key element in getting people to drive or fly out to your event. Also, make sure the venue offers you the refreshments, audiovisual, and room types you need to pull off a successful event.

This chapter also covers how to evaluate the venue options to ensure a good flow pattern exists between the rooms for easy transitions. It will help guide you through arranging for additional supplies, such as a computer or a notebook and pen for each person. Additionally, this chapter helps you think about the food, refreshments, and break-room options for attendees, staff, and speakers.

How to Choose the Best Date

The first item to start researching is the best date or dates for hosting your event. It is best to not select dates and days of the week for your event randomly. Although you can select dates to start randomly, spend some time researching these dates before moving forward. Some of the calendar items to consider include the other local and competing events taking place on the same dates. You also want to be mindful of holidays and high-cost times for travel for those attendees who need to pay for a form of transportation and possibly even lodging for the event.

Also, consider the days of the weeks you want to host your event. Depending on the audience, a specific day or days of the week might be more convenient than others. For example, a workshop for teachers might best be scheduled for weekends when educators do not work. On the other hand, a seminar for vendors in the wedding-planning business is best scheduled for weekdays because the majority of these vendors work events on the weekend.

Research local and competing events

Pull up the community calendar for your local geographic region or the region in which you are hosting the event. These calendars are online, in local newspapers, in regional magazines, and even on television listings during news broadcasts. Locate the events taking place on the same dates and during the same times you are thinking of planning your event. Consider:

- Is the audience attending these events the same as the audience that would attend your event?

- Can you combine efforts with an existing event to piggyback on the audience the event is attracting, or is it a direct competition?

- What can you do to draw the audience away from the competition? In other words, what differentiates your event from the other one?

- Is it better to choose another date?

- Can you choose times that are not conflicting with the other event but still conducive for the audience and your event needs?

Events take place almost every day of the year, so you would never be able to plan your event if you try to schedule it for a date when nothing else is happening. Instead, shoot for the best dates and times, which are those that do not have any events directly competing with yours.

Consider more than local events. Find events that attract the same audience across the country and even those that might garner the attention of your audience in other parts of the world. If your event is big enough or the topic is popular enough to attract people from other states or even countries, then your research on competing events should extend accordingly. You also want to be aware of any organizations that are hosting events similar to your own so that you are not competing for the audience.

Be aware of holidays

After researching the local events taking place, your next step should be to look at the holiday schedule. It is not a good idea to plan an event surrounding any major federal or religious holidays. It is especially important to be aware of holidays that pertain to your target audience. For example, if your event is for the United Kingdom (UK) market, then research dates on the British calendar more so than the American calendar. If the event location is in the U.S. but you still are hoping to attract a UK target audience, look at both calendars because you need to plan for your audience to travel to the U.S.

If you are targeting audiences from various countries, locate calendars that relate to the industry professionals or attendees you are targeting. For example, if your audience is geothermal engineers, then pull industry, association, and organization calendars of events on geothermal topics that would attract geothermal engineers. Although you are not going to be able to find every event that might lure your audience members away from your event, be as comprehensive as possible to ensure you are not in direct competition with a similar event.

Travel costs

Certain times of the year have higher costs for travel than others. Some of the costs even vary in different parts of the country. For example, when it is spring break or winter, travel to warmer parts of the country tends to be more expensive.

If you are responsible for booking and paying for attendees to come to your seminar or workshop, consider travel costs as part of the budget. If the attendees are responsible for booking and paying for their own travel, travel is still something you want to consider. If it is cost prohibitive for attendees to get to your event, you are going to have low attendance. If the cost to travel is low or average, you are likely to have higher attendance as long as the other factors fall into place.

Tips for choosing productive dates and times for seminars and workshops:

- Consider rush hour and traffic in the area where you are hosting the seminar or workshop. Try to set start and end times so that participants can avoid rush hour when they are trying to get to the event or leave the event.

- Consider your audience. If you are hosting an event for business professionals, then schedule an event starting at 8 a.m. and ending at 4 p.m. because this is in line with their normal working schedule. If you are targeting nannies or stay-at-home moms, then you might want to consider a later start time to give them enough time to get the kids to school and day care. Whoever your audience members are, try to work in the time that is as close to their current schedule as possible. This helps increase the attendance at your event, and it also helps increase the productivity of the attendees because they are learning during their normal schedule.

- If you are hosting a workshop or seminar that is set to last half the day, work within the timeframe of 8 a.m. to 12:30 p.m. or from 12:30 p.m. to 5 p.m.

- If you are hosting a seminar or workshop for the whole day, make sure that you start the event by 9 a.m. and end it no later than 5 p.m.

- If you are hosting an event where attendees are flying in and arriving from other parts of the country, it is likely a multiday event. To help with travel situations, you should end the final day of the seminar no later than 4 p.m. By the end, people like to fly out and leave at a decent hour, so they can get home at a decent hour.

- For evening seminars, plan to start and end between 6:30 p.m. and 9:30 p.m. This allows attendees to eat dinner before the event but still leave and get home before it gets too late.

- When you have a lot of content to deliver, multiple days might be necessary. The best practice is to shorten the number of days of the event as much as possible. You can make the session days longer, but still reduce the total number of days. This works better because attendees have an easier time devoting two eight-hour days to the event than they do three four-hour sessions per day.

- Seminars and workshops of a personal nature should be scheduled during evenings on the weekdays. This permits attendees to participate in the event without having work conflicts.

- Business seminars and workshops should end in the early afternoon. This permits business professionals to get back to their office or end the day at a decent hour.

Setting the Agenda and Time Period

Also, work out the times for the event. Choosing times can get tricky, depending on the type of workshop or seminar you are planning. For example, a seminar might just be a one- or two-hour event. Other seminars might have multiple sessions taking place simultaneously or in back-to-back sessions. You want the length of each day of the event to be long enough to fit everything in for that day. Each session should be long enough to cover the material but not so long that you lose the attention of the audience.

Again, there are several factors to consider. The first is your attendees. If attendees are local and are taking public transportation or driving in, you might opt to start and end the seminar before traffic starts in the morning and evening commute. For attendees who are flying in for a multiple-day event and staying at the same hotel where the seminars and workshops are, make the start times earlier and the end times later because commuting and traffic are not factors.

Besides the attendees, also consider times that are convenient and available at the venue. Most hotels and resorts are flexible, but they have to have staff on hand to run your event.

At this point, you will be setting a tentative agenda based on the research you have done, the topics you have set, and the formats you have chosen. The easiest way is to book things into one-hour time slots. For example, have the check-in time for attendees start at 8 a.m. and run until 9 a.m. Then you might schedule the main speaker or keynote speaker from 9 a.m. to 10 a.m. After this, you can divide the audience into small groups for breakout sessions in individual rooms. These time slots also might be for one hour each. The sessions might need to run concurrent to one another, so you might have to schedule several time slots for the same sessions to allow each attendee to choose the slots they want to attend.

Having all this information sketched out helps you narrow down the options for the venues or locations to consider. The layout and availability of the types of rooms and space you need become important in your search.

How to create a preliminary room setup

Remember the formats you learned about at the end of Chapter 1. Once you have the formats of each session thought out, it is time to sketch out the room and event layout or floor plan. If you have a venue booked or a specific venue in mind, you can obtain floor plans from the venue to draw in tables, chairs, audiovisual equipment, stages, and any other equipment or needs directly on the floor plan.

If you do not have a venue in mind, your sketches will help you narrow down your venue choices to fit your needs. Alternately, your sketches will need to be adjusted to fit the location you end up using. The degree of modifications depends on how similar or different the venue is from what you used in your planning.

Check-in location

A primary check-in location should be established so that you have a central point for all the attendees to check in on arrival. The primary check-in location provides a place where attendees can pick up all the information they need to maneuver through the seminar and workshop session or sessions. Checking in should be fast, simple, and easy for attendees. Additionally, the check-in provides the host with the opportunity to determine who is in attendance, who registered but did not come, and who registered at the door instead of ahead of time.

If your event has multiple sessions, you might want to consider having a check-in location for each separate session. These check-ins should be in addition to the primary check-in. For attendees that had to preregister for the session, this is a way of taking attendance. For events in which attendees can choose sessions according to their own schedules, this is a good way to determine attendance as well because they preregister for the sessions.

Seating arrangements

Seating arrangements are another important factor in choosing a date, time, and place for your event. If you need one large ballroom for the keynote speaker that holds upward of 200 people, find a venue that can hold a stage and the number of chairs.

Requiring attendees to preregister for the event helps you to better plan for seating up front. You will know how many tables, chairs, computers, tablets, or other items you will need. You always can bring a few extras for those who register at the door. If you do not require some type of preregistration process, then you still will need to estimate attendance or limit the number of people in each session based on the space you have.

Here is a sample agenda to give you an idea of how you might plan the time slots for your own event.

Friday, July 12, 2013	
12 noon – 1 p.m.	Frieda Gleeker: Keynote Speaker and Keynote Address
1 p.m. – 2 p.m.	Breakout Session A — Group 1
1 p.m. – 2 p.m.	Breakout Session B — Group 2
2:15 p.m. – 2:30 p.m.	Break
3:30 p.m. – 4 p.m.	Break & Networking Session
4 p.m. – 5 p.m.	Breakout Session A — Group 2
4 p.m. – 5 p.m.	Breakout Session B — Group 1
5 p.m. – 5:15 p.m.	Break
5:15 p.m. – 6:15 p.m.	Panel Discussion
Saturday, July 13, 2013	
8 a.m. – 9 a.m.	Gina Jenkins: Motivational Speaker
9 a.m. – 10:15 a.m.	Breakout Session A — Group 1
9 a.m. – 10:15 a.m.	Breakout Session B — Group 2
10:15 a.m. – 10:30 a.m.	Break
10:30 a.m. – 11 a.m.	Breakout Session A — Group 2
10:30 a.m. – 11 a.m.	Breakout Session B — Group 1
11 a.m. – 12 noon	Panel Discussion
12 noon – 1:30 p.m.	Lunch Break
1:30 p.m. – 2:30 p.m.	Breakout Session C — Group 1
1:30 p.m. – 2:30 p.m.	Breakout Session D — Group 2
2:30 p.m. – 3:30 p.m.	Breakout Session C — Group 2
2:30 p.m. – 3:30 p.m.	Breakout Session D — Group 1
3:30 p.m. – 4 p.m.	Closing Session

Location is Everything

The location of the event should fit your needs and wants and be attractive to the audience. Some conferences sell out or increase attendance rates because of the location of the event. A Las Vegas event might sell out for almost any industry or topic, while the same industry or topic conference in Idaho might struggle to fill the spots.

"Curb appeal," or locations that are attractive to audience members, is one way to measure the effectiveness of a certain location. You also have to choose hotels, resorts, clubhouses, or other venues that are the right fit for the type of event you are hosting.

Finding the right fit requires you to first evaluate the number and type of rooms available. Then, you have to evaluate how to use the space. Last, it requires you to determine if the space allows for the transitions you need to make. This last consideration is for conferences, seminars, and workshops that require attendees to move between sessions.

Evaluating number of rooms available

The first stop is to determine the number of rooms you will need for each aspect of your event. If you are hosting one topic, then you might only need one room at a local hotel or venue. If you have multiple topics running simultaneously, however, you will need a venue that possesses several different rooms. In some circumstances with a larger number of attendees, you will need one large ballroom area for the keynote speaker and then smaller conference rooms or breakout rooms for the sessions that follow the keynote speaker.

The number of rooms you need directly affects the venues you put on your search list and the venues that make the final cut. For example, you might consider renting a women's club for your event. The club has one large room that holds 150 people seated at chairs and tables. The club has an unstaffed kitchen, a storage room, and one small room off the ballroom that holds 20 people seated with tables. Because your seminar includes a keynote speaker that will speak to all the attendees at once and you do not plan to serve food and refreshments, the club is ideal for your event.

Also, note any requirements you have for storage. For the example event at the women's club, you can store your handouts and marketing materials in the storage room so that everything is out of the way and not cluttering the main speaking area. For check-in, you decide to place a small table and chair at the entrance so that as soon as attendees walk in the door, the check-in table is the first thing they see.

In short, create a checklist of the space needs you have for your event. Also, add to the list any amenities or extras you need the venue to offer. Otherwise, they will have to allow you to bring in, rent, or buy these supplies from another company. At this point, this is a working checklist. Have the basic structure of the checklist together, but as you continue to plan the seminar and workshop, continuously add items to this list. For now, know:

- How many rooms you need for the event

- The approximate size or number of people each room should hold

- The format and setup style for each event to ensure the space accommodates you

- Some of the amenities you need, such as refreshment services, the availability of tables, chairs, and linens as part of the setup, and audiovisual equipment

- The ability to bring in any items or service providers that the venue does not provide

Evaluating space

With your preliminary venue checklist in hand, start researching venues that provide the items you know you need at this point. Most venues do not provide pricing on their website or on the phone, so schedule appointments to view the venue and speak with one of the venue coordinators who will assess your needs and provide you with a price proposal. When you go to your appointment, take the checklist with you. Make sure you have something to write with as well.

As you start to view venues, this is a prime time to add to your checklist. The venue coordinators will ask about your needs and wants for the event. This questioning often leads to a realization of some of the other items and services that should be a part of your checklist.

The goal is to narrow down the venues to the ones that fit all or the majority of your needs and wants.

Room flow for easy transitions

For seminars and workshops that have multiple rooms and sessions, review the flow between the rooms as well. If you have 200 people coming out of the main room and heading to the smaller breakout rooms, does the hallway allow for easy transition, or is the hallway going to get clogged with people trying to get from one room to another?

Also, evaluate the space the hallways and corridors provide in between each room. Is there enough room for attendees to flow in simultaneously without having to feel as if they are in a cattle herd?

If your venue rents out space for more than one event at a time, factor this into your transition evaluation. Try to determine how many people are expected to be coming in and leaving during the same time that your attendees are arriving or transitioning from each room.

Services and rentals

As you are evaluating the venues, also determine the services and rentals the venue offers. As you are walking through the venue and meeting with the event coordinator, talk about each item or service. Read the following sections to find out what items and services about which to ask.

Some venues include the item or service in the cost for renting the space. Other locations charge extra for each service or item you require. Also, find out what items the venue allows you to bring in because some locations prohibit off-site vendors from providing specific items. For example, you might want to bring in your own bagels and coffee for a two-hour breakfast seminar. However, the hotel where you are renting the room might not allow outside food or beverages.

Food is one example of the items and services to find out about when evaluating a venue or space.

Computer or writing instruments for each person

Depending on the type of seminars and workshops you are hosting, you might want to consider providing a computer, tablet, or notepads and pens to each of the attendees. Venues, especially the large ones, often have on-site audiovisual departments, so

you can rent computers and tablets for each attendee to get the most out of their time at the event. Again, for even the venues that have the option to rent these items, it might not be as cost-effective as renting these items from an external or third-party provider. To make a proper price comparison, find out if it is possible for you to arrange for these items to be brought to the event or if you have to use the on-site department.

In addition to price, convenience is another aspect to consider. When you can arrange for any extra items you might need with the venue, you only have to work with one point of contact during the planning process instead of coordinating with multiple people.

Microphones and audio equipment

When you are speaking to larger groups, the availability of microphones, amplifiers, speakers, and other audio equipment is important. Most larger hotels, conference centers, and venues offer these items à la carte. When you are working with smaller hotels, clubs, and smaller venues, they might not offer these types of services on site. When the venue does not offer the audiovisual equipment you require, you can bring in a third-party venue to provide what you need. Verify this with the venue, however, to ensure that you will not run into problems.

Chairs

It might sound like a basic item, but every seminar and workshop needs chairs. You need chairs for your attendees. You require chairs for speakers and teachers. You even need chairs for the event staff that works the information and check-in tables. Some venues have chairs on site that are part of the room rental or that you can pay to use during your event. If your chosen venue does not have chairs to offer, you will have to rent chairs from a party rental or chair rental company.

Tables

Even if you are setting up the room with chairs for attendees and the speaker will be using a microphone at the front of the room, you need a table to use as a check-in desk. You also might want tables on which to display information at the back of the room. If you only need a table for check-in purposes, you might consider bringing in your own folding table that you cover with linens.

The shape of the tables might also be a factor. Rectangular tables are more appropriate for certain setup situations, such as when attendees only need to listen to a speaker, but round tables are better for other circumstances, such as discussions and interactions. The shape of the table directly correlates with the format for your event. For example, in a workshop in which you want all 20 people to interact with one another for a panel discussion, you might want to set up rectangular tables to form a "U" or "L" shape. If the same session requires attendees to break up into groups of ten, you might want to have two round ten-person tables in the room.

Linens

Table covers, chair covers, and possibly even linen napkins are other items you might need. Some tables rented out by venues and even party rental companies are made of plywood, so they are not presentable as is. You most likely will need to cover each table with a table cover. You can rent wooden or other types of tables that do not require linen covers, but this is more expensive than renting a standard table and cover.

Chairs can go either way. Some banquet chairs are presentable as they are. If you are trying to dress up a chair or it is more of a formal event, you might want to rent linen chair covers. Linen napkins fall into the same category. If you are hosting a formal luncheon seminar, then splurging to rent linen napkins takes the event up a notch from providing paper, disposable napkins with the meal.

Food service

Food and beverage service tends to be a big part of seminars and workshops. This is especially true for seminars and workshops that are all-day or multiple-day events. Often, part of the registration fee that attendees pay for includes refreshments, snacks, and even full meals.

Food and beverage offerings can be simple or more complex. The venue might have the ability to put out snacks and refreshments to keep it on the simple side. They might be able to accommodate a sit-down served meal, in which they provide the food, beverages, and wait staff to serve the meal.

Although the wants you have for the event are one thing, what you truly need and can afford is something else. *In Chapter 3, you will learn how to translate these individual items and services into a budget.*

Chapter Three

Creating a Budget

One of the most important elements to create for your seminar is the budget so that you know exactly how much money to have on hand for everything it takes to pull off the big day. Creating a budget also allows you to price tickets or admission fees to cover these costs and make money off your seminar. A sample budget and list of line items to consider are also included in the chapter.

How to Create a Budget

When you are building your event budget, you have different options. You might have a total amount you can spend on the event. Using this lump-sum figure, you can work backward to assign a spending limit to each line item. The other option in

building a budget is to estimate a cost for each item and service. Total the cost of each item to get the total cost estimate for hosting the event.

The process you use for creating a budget often depends on the type of event you are hosting. In other words, it goes back to the purpose of the event. A professional organization hosting its annual conference for members has a budget to spend on the event because it allocates a certain percentage of member fees. In this case, the planner for the organization has a lump-sum amount he or she has available to spend on putting on the event.

When an industry expert is hosting an informational seminar or workshop and is selling tickets for the event, the cost of these tickets should cover the expenses of the event. Additionally, the expert might price the tickets to profit off the ticket sales. Once the event host knows how much the event will cost, then he or she can price the tickets to cover the cost and profit from the event.

When you are building the budget, find a system that works for you. You can use an old-fashioned paper and pencil, or you can go modern and build a budget in a spreadsheet program. Whatever option you choose, it is easier to build a budget by dividing the budget into rows and columns.

The columns to create include:

- Item or service description
- Estimated cost
- Actual cost
- Difference
- Totals

Each row is one line item or item/service description. For example, a budget worksheet might look like this:

Description	Estimated Cost	Actual Cost	Difference	Totals
Room rental	$1,500	$1,250	($250)	$1,250
Tables	$550	$550	$0	$550
Table covers	$300	$275	($25)	$275
Total				**$2,075**

Sample budget

Next, you will find a sample budget for hosting a seminar or workshop. Use the sample budget as a guide for creating your own budget. Reviewing the sample budget will help you determine some of the items, services, products, and costs you might be thinking of at this point in the planning process. However, no two event budgets are alike; each event has slightly different needs and wants. You can use the sample budget as a guide to get a good idea of how to build your own event budget.

Sample budget

Expenses per Person	Per Person	Total Cost Per Person	Number of Attendees	Admission Fee per person
1. Name badge and holder	$0.50	$79.00	125	$112.52
2. Continental Breakfast	$12.00		150	$107.27
3. Lunch	$17.50		200	$100.20

4. Dinner	$25.00			
5. Snack Breaks	$10.00			
6. Workshop notebook and bags	$5.00			
7. Handouts/worksheets/agendas	$5.50			
8. Session and conference evaluation forms	$0.50			
9. Credit card processing fee	$3.00			
Expenses	**Flat Rate**			
10. Keynote Speaker speaking fee	$1,070.00			
11. Keynote speaker hotel, travel, and meals	$650.00			
12. Promotional products	$20.00			
13. Audiovisual rentals	$1,500			
14. Room rental fees	$2,000.00			
15. Signs	$250.00			

Tracking expenses

When you create your budget sheet, add a column next to each expense estimate for actual expense. Before you spend money on buying or renting a product or service, review your budget. Ideally, do not spend more than what you have budgeted for the item. Whatever the cost is to you, add this figure to the actual expense column so you can keep track of where you are in your spending.

Tracking expenses as you go helps you stay within your budget. Additionally, tracking expenses gives you an opportunity to reallocate funds as necessary. For example, if you end up saving money on one area, you either can save this money or allocate it to an area of the budget that ended up costing you more money than you originally budgeted.

CASE STUDY: SET THE BUDGET FOR A SUCCESSFUL EVENT

Griot's Roll Film Production
& Services Inc.
Eula M. Young, COO
276 West 135th Street
Suite 4A
New York, NY 10030
(212) 281-2286
www.griotsrollproduction.com

Griot's Roll Film Production & Services Inc. is a video marketing company that provides video services for businesses, nonprofits, corporations, and city and state agencies. These clients are looking to demonstrate a product, educate their target market on their services, or an organization looking to improve their online presence using video and social media. Griot's Roll creates the online video for the clients, as well as helps clients create a marketing and advertising campaign surrounding the video. Griot's Roll tracks the campaigns success through the uses of video analytics and other tracking and data software.

Using seminars and workshops is a great way to establish the brand and as a marketing tool to gain exposure. Griot's Roll uses networking/seminars to expose the company to a wider audience and to educate small business owners and entrepreneurs on how to use marketing to build their brand, using video and other online tools to promote their businesses. By adding the seminar piece to an existing networking strategy, the company was able to build a brand and gave them a platform for meeting potential customers. Since the company's target market is midsize to large businesses, and corporation, Griot's Roll uses partnerships and experts to that come to their events as discussion panelists to help educate the consumer.

The seminar objective is to help small business owners meet their media needs, so that they will have the ability to compete with their competition. Griot's Roll teaches attendees about the marketing tools that work and how to use these tools to succeed. Specifically, the seminars teach attendees how to use media online to level the playing field between small businesses and their large counterparts.

Griot's Roll hosts its seminars for a very specific target market. The profile of the networking/seminar attendees are startup business owners and entrepreneurs who have been in business for under five years and are trying to figure out how to grow their business and stay in business. Their gross revenue is less than $50,000 annually.

Depending on the costs to host the event, the networking/seminars usually little to no cost to the attendee because the company is not trying to make money from the events, but rather trying to educate these business owners on the services Griot's Roll can provide.

Another target market for the seminars are corporations, city and state agencies, and midsize to large organizations that spend more than $50,000 a year in advertising and marketing. These companies have been in existence for more than ten years, and they know what it takes to get the word out about their brand. They are looking for experts in this field, and they know it will take money to build their brand. These are the decision makers, and they are often on the panels or speaking at the event. For these decision makers, the education angle is about the results they can achieve to reach their target market.

Setting the budget for each event depends on the cost for the venue, food, printing, signage, and other expenses. Griot's Roll builds the budget from the ground up, finding out the estimate of costs before setting the cost for attendees. The company has funds allocated in its budget for these events. If the event price falls within the budget, or if the company experts are speaking at someone else's event, then the events are at no cost to attendees. If costs exceed the budget, then a fee for attendance is charged. Logistics and location are key points in figuring out a budget. If the venue is expensive, then it raises the cost of the event. The area where the event is located also affects the costs, such as catering and the experts that speak at the event. Planning for an event usually takes four to six months

Setting Ticket and Admission Prices

You can use the cost of the event that you approximate in your budget to set the ticket and admission prices. First, look at the costs of the event. Then, decide how much of a profit you want to make. There is no typical profit margin, so it is up to you how much of an up-charge you want to add onto the ticket prices. On the other hand, however, you want to set ticket prices that are affordable and comparable to what other events are charging. If you have to price your fees higher than similar events to cover the costs for hosting the event, consider evaluating ways to cut down or cut out expenses. You want to find the right balance of making money and staying competitive.

Some pricing strategies to consider include early-bird specials, full-ticket admission, partial-ticket admission, à la carte pricing, and pricing any products or services you sell during the event.

Early-bird specials

Early-bird specials are prices provided to those who register for the event early. A rule of thumb is to offer a 10- to 15-percent discount off the regular price. For example, if the registration fee is $95, then early birds can register for $80.75.

What you consider "early" is relative. For a smaller event that does not have a long lead time, you might offer early-bird pricing for those who register three to four weeks before the workshop or seminar. For bigger conferences and events that take longer to plan, early-bird specials might run a year in advance up to a few months before the conference start date.

When setting your early-bird pricing, also include the deadline for enjoying the early-bird special. This creates some urgency for attendees to preregister for the event. When they preregister for the event, you get their money up front, so you have money in your pocket to pay for the expenses of hosting the event, and you start to get a good idea of how many attendees you can expect. It is not unheard of for events to sell out or come close to selling out during the early-bird registration period. Because you should have a venue booked at this point, the number of attendees the venue can hold limits your cap. If you have more people who want to register, find out if your venue has additional space available. This will determine what the cap of attendees is for your event.

Full-ticket admission

When you have a workshop or seminar that is multiple days or has various portions, you might want to break the admission fees up. A full-ticket admission permits attendees to attend any and all the information sessions they wish. It also provides access to the trade show floor if you have vendors set up to share information with the attendees. A full-admission ticket also would provide access to all or some of the meals you provide.

Of all the ticket prices, the full-ticket admission price is the highest. This is because it is an all-access ticket. If your event has social components or special components, such as formal dinners or served luncheons with the speakers, you can provide these components as à la carte add-ons, which are discussed more thoroughly in the à la carte pricing section of this chapter.

Partial-ticket admission

Another pricing option for admission is a partial-ticket admission price. Partial-ticket admission provides access to some of the seminars and workshops but limits the access to just these events. For example, a partial-ticket admission would provide access to the informational sessions but would not provide access to the trade show room floor or the meals. Because of the limited amount of access, the ticket price is less expensive than tickets that have full access to everything the event has to offer.

If the full-ticket admission price is $95, a partial-ticket price might be $75 or less. To determine how much of a discount you can provide, return to your budget to calculate how much the cost is per person for the portions of the event to which you are giving them access. To break even, charge at least what the cost is to you. If you want to turn a profit, charge more than the cost to you.

À la carte pricing

A third option for pricing is the à la carte option. Event hosts use à la carte pricing for add-ons to the full- or partial-ticket admission price. For events that have after-hour cocktail parties, formal dinners, and other social events, attendees can opt to participate in these events. It is a "pay-to-play"-type option.

You also might choose an à la carte pricing strategy for seminars and workshops with multiple components. For example, you might charge attendees, who wish to attend the session to hear the keynote speaker but do not wish to participate in the breakout sessions, just the amount of money due for the keynote speaker.

At-the-door prices

If you have slots to fill on the day or days of the event, you also might wish to price "at-the-door" admissions. People who pay as they arrive pay more than those who preregister for the event. Use your discretion in making this decision. For example, if the person comes on the third day of a three-day event, then charging them more than a three-day admission price is not fair or wise.

You also might consider that any money you make on the day of an event is money you did not have yesterday. This might cause you to price the admission at the same or less than preregistration prices. On the other hand, you might not want to do this because it does not provide an incentive to preregister when it comes to hosting future events.

Ways to Increase Income

To turn a profit, you have to sell tickets for more than it costs to host the event. In addition, you have to sell enough admission tickets to cover more than your total costs. However, selling admission to the event is not the only option you have for making money. You also have the option of selling products, services, memberships, or even admission to your future events.

If you intend to sell any of your products or services at the event, consider offering some type of a special on any products or services. This strategy gives attendees an incentive to buy then instead of deciding to buy later. Let them know that if they buy your product or service at the event, they are getting a special price.

You can decide what type of a discount you want to offer. Just make sure you still are turning a profit on the product or service when selling it at the cheaper price.

Sell products

The products you choose to sell can run the gamut. You might be an expert in your field and have informational products to sell. Informational products consist of books, DVDs, CDs, workbooks, home study courses, and packages of information that you can package and sell at the event. For example, if you are a small business coach talking about writing a business plan, you can sell a home study course on building a business plan. Even though the marketing plan is a part of the business plan, it is such a large and important part of the business plan that you might sell a separate home study course that focuses specifically on writing the marketing plan.

Products also might be literal products. The commercial cleaning company hosting a seminar about creating a green working environment might sell its line of green cleaning products at the event, for example.

When selling products at a seminar or workshop, this is an indirect sell, meaning the products are sold at the back of the room. The primary purpose of the event is to lead attendees in with the information you and any experts speaking at your event have to offer. Once you build trust and credibility with your audience, then you can offer the products as a last-minute sell as the event is wrapping up.

Sell services

The service you choose to sell at events can run the spectrum, too. You might be an expert in your field and offer your service menu as a follow-up to the information you shared with them during your session or sessions. For example, a mortgage broker might host a seminar on pitfalls to avoid when refinancing a home. The ultimate goal of the mortgage broker is to get the audience member to use the mortgage broker's service to refinance one or more of his or her properties.

Services also might be more literal. The commercial cleaning company might sell its cleaning services at the event in addition to the products. A personal trainer might sell personal training session packages, along with vitamins and supplements to help individuals reach their weight, nutrition, and fitness goals. As with the products, selling your services is an indirect sell.

Sell memberships

For events that membership organizations host, this is a prime time to sell memberships. First, consider offering existing members the chance to renew their memberships at a special show price. Second, this is a good time to recruit new members. You can show them that one of the biggest benefits of being a member is the information and educational resources your organization provides because they are experiencing it firsthand by attending the event. Again, you can sell these introductory memberships at a reduced rate if they register at the show.

Sell admission to future events

Current events are also prime times to sell admission to future events. At an annual conference, for example, you can presell registration to the next annual conference. This gives you a head start on selling admission tickets filling seats for the following year. If you are hosting seminars and workshops, you can sell admission to any upcoming events you have. You might want to provide an incentive by offering a discount if they register then. You also can send them away with the registration information, so if they register later, they pay full price.

CASE STUDY: LEVERAGE KNOWLEDGE TO SELL

EGT Global Trading
Edie Tolchin a.k.a. "The Sourcing Lady"[SM]
P. O. Box 231
Florida, NY 10921
(845) 321-2362
www.egtglobaltrading.com

EGT Global Trading provides product development services for inventors and innovators with new products. Services include product safety and Consumer Product Safety Improvement Act services, China sourcing and manufacturing, quality control, production testing, shipping and import arrangements, and legally importing clients' products into the USA and throughout the world. Baby and children's products are a specialty of EGT Global Trading and its owner, Edie Tolchin, because of myriad safety issues affecting these types of products.

Because Tolchin works mainly with inventors and entrepreneurs who are launching new products, her mission is to provide information on how to manufacture a safe product while working with foreign factories where there might be communication issues or other challenges, such as product safety, quality control, etc. These seminars are provided free of charge to inventor groups (who typically have monthly meetings) or at trade shows catering to inventions and new products.

Tolchin has 35 years of experience in importing, export, and manufacturing and EGT Global Trading has been in business for 15 years. With all of her experience, she has a very good idea of the type of crowd attending the events. She typically coordinates with the president of the group the type of program they would like. Hot topics in the inventions industry that directly relate to the services Tolchin provides include, "Making a SAFE Product in China" or "Importing A to Z," among many others. If it is a trade show, she normally speaks with the directors to see which of several seminars she can provide. Another topic Tolchin finds is a good foundation for her educational talk is her book, "Sourcing Smarts: Keeping it SIMPLE and SAFE with China Sourcing and Manufacturing."

When the book is the basis of her discussion, Tolchin typically promotes the book throughout the seminar. Since most of her seminars and workshops are about product safety, sourcing, and manufacturing in China, her book is a natural fit. Tolchin always has copies of the book at a table near the podium. She shows the audience the book and tells them the books are available for purchase and signing after the seminar.

Tolchin usually brings someone with her to help man the table, but sometimes she does it alone. In addition to selling the books in her seminar room, she also sells the book at other places during the event. For example at **www.inpex.com**, where she sometimes presents at their seminars, Tolchin serves at their Resource Center (where professionals sit in an assigned area and take appointments and walk-ins from people seeking advice). Tolchin also uses this opportunity to promote her book as well.

The group hosting the event covers most of the expenses required for seminars, workshops, and trade shows where Tolchin speaks. For example, if it is a trade show, the group usually covers travel expenses, such as lodging, shuttle services, food, etc. Most groups also print handouts of the PowerPoint® presentations Tolchin normally uses and provides all audiovisual requirements, such as media projector, laptop, etc. She does not charge an honorarium for speaking.

Tolchin's mission is to get the word out about product safety. In the inventions and China manufacturing industry, the average inventor has little, if no, knowledge of how to make products overseas safely and how to work with a foreign factory, among many other things. Her primary goal in speaking at these events to educate attendees, position herself as an expert, and convince the attendees that she is the professional they should use as sourcing and product safety consultant. Tolchin always tries to come away with a new client or two from the sessions, too. Since each client project usually yields between $10K and $12K, sometimes even $15K for the duration of the project, she deems her talk a success if she walks away with at least one new client.

Once you have the beginning stages of your event in place, it is time to start thinking about all the professionals you need to hire. *In Chapter 4, you will uncover all the details of establishing the event team of professionals to help you pull off the event.*

Chapter Four

Establishing Your Team of Professionals

In Chapter 4, you will discover how to find all the people you need to plan and implement your event. This includes staff to run the event, such as people to check in attendees and hand out information packets. This chapter also covers how to find and book speakers and professionals in your industry to conduct the workshops that are a part of your conference.

Hiring Staff to Plan the Event

Although you have everything you need in this book to plan your own workshops and seminars, you do have the option of hiring a professional planner to take care of all the details for you. These professionals handle all the details on your behalf. Because  these professionals plan events on a regular basis, they already have a pool of vendors, venues, and ideas they can pull from to plan your workshop or seminar faster and easier than you might be able to do on your own.

On the other hand, hiring a professional planner might increase your expenses. Professional meeting and event planners charge a fee for their services. You might pay an hourly rate, a flat fee, or a percentage of your event budget to the planner. However, the planner might be able to negotiate better pricing with venues and vendors than you would be able to obtain on your own. In this case, the amount of money a professional planner saves you might be more than enough to make up for the fee you have to pay for their services.

Ask for referrals for event planners, meeting planners, or coordinators from other professionals you know that host seminars and workshops. You also can ask for referrals from hotels and other locations because they often maintain a list of professionals who might be able to help you with your event. You can also turn to Internet and the listings in the Yellow Pages®.

Once you have a list of potential event planners, your work is just beginning. Start by conducting online research about the planning company. Find out if they specialize in a particular type of event, such as seminars or workshops, and uncover whether the planner specializes in any type of industry. For example, some planner might specialize in planning real estate and mortgage events or bridal shows. If the planner has industry experience in your industry, it can benefit your event.

Narrow down your choices. Contact each planner and schedule a face-to-face or phone interview. Talk with the representative of the planning company to discuss his or her experience in planning the specific type of event you are hosting. Gather pricing. For any planners who were not referred to you, obtain at least three client references.

Contact each of the references. Find out what that person's experience was working with the planner. Find out the advantages and disadvantages the client had with the planner. All this information helps you narrow down the options of the planners who are best suited to help you plan your seminar or workshop.

Once you decide on the planning company you want to work with, put your working agreement in writing. All professional planners have a contract or agreement that spells out the details of your working relationship, pricing, services they will provide, and various other details about your working relationship. Read the agreement carefully and make sure everything you discuss is included in the written contract before signing it and giving the planner a deposit.

Contracts with Vendors

Vendors provide the supplies and services that keep your event running smoothly. Just as with every aspect of business, building solid relationships with suppliers is the path to long-term event success and profitability. If you earn your vendor's trust over time, they may be willing to help you out during those hopefully rare times when your bank account is squeezed. On the other hand, you do not want to rely too heavily on the good will of your vendors, especially early in your relationship, or overpromise your potential value as a customer to them. Mutual respect between a vendor and you as customer is the goal.

What types of vendors will your events need to function? Most events, seminars, workshops, and conferences need general services, such as the local media or ad agencies that run the event advertising programs. If you create and buy advertising, the printer who prints your fliers is another business events use. Your phone service, your Internet service provider, and website developer are but a few of the other types of vendors you will need to work with on an ongoing basis to produce your events and programs.

Some of these vendors may offer you special commercial contracts, viewing you as a fellow professional in the business. There are many advantages to arranging a commercial account, including discounts in some cases, but you may have to negotiate this with someone beyond the sales clerk level to get your business plugged into the system. Usually, you have to supply banking and credit references, which are sometimes difficult to obtain when you are just starting out.

If you have good credit, you may be able to establish a line of credit with important vendors, allowing you to charge the goods or materials you need for your customers and pay in 30 days. This is a distinct advantage for you, because the supplier carries your up-front cost while you take care of your customer. Then when you make money from selling admission to the event, collecting dues, or selling product or services at the seminar, workshop, or conference, then you subsequently can pay each of the vendors that helped you put the event on to start.

A purchase order is a contract you make with a vendor that specifies exactly what and to whom the material is to be given. There are several advantages in using purchase orders. By officially giving notice to your vendors that you always will supply a purchase order for any charge, you will avoid mistakes that might permit an unauthorized person to wrongly bill a purchase to your account. Purchase orders also provide complete records of transactions with individual vendors, so you easily can track how much of a particular product you buy. Because purchase order numbers are noted on vendor invoicing, all cost changes will be monitored easily, too. Even if your credit history does not give you the option to set up commercial accounts immediately when you open, you still can start your seminar and workshop business. You should simply expect to "pay retail" until you can demonstrate to your vendors that you are seriously engaged in business and will be a profitable customer for them in the end.

Another way many businesses, associations, and organizations start hosting events, seminars, workshops, and conferences is use national credit cards, such as MasterCard®, Visa®, or Discover®. Credit card interest rates are usually higher than individual vendor credit lines, and the opportunity to build a close vendor/customer relationship is less compelling, but credit cards might give you the chance to make partial payments and not pay the entire bill in 30 days. Again, this provides you with some leeway between the time you have to pay vendors and the time you have money coming in from the attendees of the event. Just be sure you pay the credit card company on time. Late fees involve serious penalties that will destroy your profitability in a hurry, while simultaneously damaging your credit rating and business reputation with vendors.

Planning by yourself

If you opt to plan the event on your own, contact the vendor, venues, and service providers on your own. You will have to conduct your own interviews, reference check, and price comparisons for each aspect of putting your event together.

For each item or service you require, obtain referrals from people who have used these service providers before. You even might be able to draw from your own experiences. For example, if you require audiovisual equipment, you might use the same company your employer uses. If you need linens, you might use the same company you rented linens from when you planned your wedding a few months before.

If you look for item and service providers in your local area via the phone book or Internet, pinpoint those that offer exactly what you need. Schedule an appointment to meet with the provider, view the products they have on display, and talk with them about their services.

When choosing vendors, use a similar process you used for choosing planners. Narrow down your choices. Talk with the representative of each company to discuss their experience in planning the specific type of event you are trying to host. Gather pricing. For any vendors that were not referred to you, obtain at least three client references from these planners.

Once you decide on the company you want to work with, put your working agreement in writing. Read this agreement carefully and make sure everything you discuss is included in the written contract before signing it and giving the vendor a deposit.

Continue this process with each line item on your budget until you have all the products and services you need for your event.

CASE STUDY: PLAN YOUR WAY TO A SUCCESSFUL EVENT

Pretty Pear Bride
Shafonne Myers
6714 Meander Run Youngstown, OH 44515
(866) 398-9041
www.prettypearbride.com

Shafonne Myers is a certified wedding and event planner who started a website for full-figured brides, **www.prettypearbride.com**. She also has a magazine for plus-size brides, which offers bridal styling and wedding planning tips. Myers uses seminars and workshops as a way to get in front of a direct target market to discuss relevant and interesting topics to them. In this case, Myers offers seminars and workshops for couples planning weddings. She supplies free information, which is what builds their trust, and then Myers is able to introduce them to services she offers.

Myers enlists her fellow wedding vendors that want to promote their services to help her put the event together, and to keep her costs as low as possible. She chooses a location that hosts weddings so that they have a chance to showcase their wares while the event is unfolding. Because the venue gains the most exposure from the event, it is standard that Myers lands the venue without paying a dime for room rental. For any extras, such as audiovisual, catering, and invitations, Myers reaches out to other wedding vendors that specialize in each of these areas to donate their products and services for their chance of getting in front of their target market. The bottom line is, this eliminates the need to have a budget for these events because each vendor is chipping in to cover the costs.

Myers sets measurable goals for the seminar or workshop on how many clients she gets from the event, as well as how many clients any of the vendors participating get from the event. She even takes it a step further and measures the number of referrals she obtains from event attendees, and how many of these referrals become clients.

Myers's primary focus is to choose which vendors she works with carefully. Because she scopes out great vendors, chooses an enticing venue, delicious caterer, and a talented florist, photography, and or stationary professional, it allows her to showcase her event planning skills for attendees to see with their own eyes and experience firsthand.

Hiring Staff to Run the Event

Now, you need to start focusing on the staff you need on the day of the event. If you run a business or work for a company, you might be able to use employees of the company to fill the roles you need. Depending on the time and day the event takes place, it might not cost you any additional money to use internal staff to help at your seminar or workshop. If the event takes place during normal working hours, staff can receive their normal salary or hourly rate for helping to staff the event. If it is off hours or on days the employees normally do not work, it might cost you overtime pay or additional pay that can rack up the expenses from your budget.

After considering the staff you have from your business or company, you might decide you need to find staff members from outside sources. Start by asking employees and people you know if they know of anyone who would be interested in working the event. You might be able to obtain teen children of employees who want to earn extra cash or possibly even credit for a class.

Another option is to post a free classified ad on sites such as Craigslist® or in the classified section of your local newspaper online. You do not have to find people who necessarily have event experience, but they should possess people and customer service skills. You always can train them on the specifics of helping to check in attendees, pass out information packets, and survey attendees about their experiences.

Although this is not a comprehensive list, and your need for staff might vary by event, some of the staff you might need to pull off your event include:

- Check-in staff (one or multiple people, depending on the number of attendees)

- Individual workshop or seminar check-in (when you have multiple sessions taking place simultaneously)

- Information desk staff

- Speaker and lecturer liaison

- Hall directors

- Survey takers

- Setup and cleanup staff

Have your staff established at least two weeks before your event. Also, consider hiring extra staff members in case one of your staff does not show up, or you determine you have an extra role you need to fill as the event unfolds.

Finding Speakers and Educational Professionals for Topics

One of the most difficult parts of staffing your event is finding the speakers and educational professionals you need for the sessions. If you are the only speaker at the event, you will have much less work to do as far as hiring is concerned. What you will need to concentrate on is putting together the presentation and materials you need to pull your own talk off with your audience. However, some of you might need to staff your convention with knowledgeable experts.

When you are researching potential topics for your events, you likely came across experts in the industry and the field. Review the sources of these topics, and do some research on their background and expertise. Experts have speaking information listed on their websites. If they do not, shoot an email or make a phone call to find out if they are available to speak at events.

Fortunately, you also can turn to find lists of speakers and resources. You can view Appendix A of this book for a list of speaker organizations. These organizations allow speakers to list their areas of expertise so you can easily find experts that cater to your needs.

Another source of speakers is professional organizations and associations. Almost every industry and profession has a professional association or organization associated with it. You can review the member listings for these organizations online or by contacting the association directly.

Hiring Speakers

Once you identify potential speakers, schedule a time to meet with or talk on the phone with the speaker or the speaker's representative. Many professional speakers have managers and public relations professionals who book their speaking engagements for them. It is possible that you will never speak with or see the speaker until he or she shows up at your event.

Some speakers speak on set topics, while others are open to working with topics you have chosen for your event. For example, a social media expert might have six different areas on his or her menu of topics. The speaker's website and informational packets provide insight into the specific details each area covers. This allows you to choose the topics that best relate to the information you want to share at your event.

Price is probably the biggest determining factor, after finding experts that can teach and speak on your topics. Most professional speakers charge for speaking at events. Professional speakers who make their living speaking at events will eat away at your budget at a much higher rate than other types of speakers. Again, you can negotiate these prices when you are talking to the speaker or their representatives.

Speakers who do not speak to earn income but to promote their business expertise speak at events on a no- or low-cost basis. These speakers are just as professional and knowledgeable as speakers that speak as their sole source of income. If the speaker does charge a fee, it is an honorarium. They might have a set fee, such as $250 or $500, or you can opt to "honor" the speaker with an amount you can afford.

When you host an event in which you have to bring speakers in from out of town, you might have additional expenses. Some speakers require the event to cover their travel, food, and hotel bills, in addition to any fees the speaker collects for speaking at the event. Find out exactly what expenses you are responsible for so you can budget accordingly. Some speakers might not expect you to pay for their expenses to travel and speak at your event. Some will do it in exchange from the publicity they get as a speaker or the opportunity they have to promote their own business. You can offer to pay some of their expenses, or pay an honorarium fee, which might be as low as $50 for their speaking time. This depends on the budget you have for the event and the negotiations you work out with the speaker. Knowing the expenses you have to cover for the speaker can make or break the speaker you choose for your event. On the other hand, a big-name speaker at your event might be able to help you draw in an even bigger crowd, which would increase ticket sales and your profit margin, ultimately providing you with more money to cover the event expenses.

Once you identify the speakers and experts you want for your event, the next step is to put your agreement in writing. Professional speakers tend to use a standard agreement that spells out what they will provide and what you are expected to provide. In other situations, you will need to use your own agreement. Be as specific as possible about what the speaker is providing, what the compensation will be, and what you intend to provide for the event. Make sure the agreement is in writing and is signed before you give a deposit or any compensation to the speaker.

Once you book a speaker, you should send a confirmation letter or email to him or her. In your confirmation, you should thank the individual for agreeing to speak at your event. Additionally, you should provide him or her with some preliminary information needed to make the event as successful for them and the attendees as possible.

A sample confirmation you might send to speakers might look something like this:

July 12, 2013

Seminars 'R Us
1234 XYZ St.
Anytown, MI USA 55555

Dear John:

Thank you again for agreeing to speak at the upcoming Seminars 'R Us event in Beverly Hills, California, on February 2. Your participation in this exciting event will add a lot of value to the event for attendees. I would like to share a few ground rules that I will provide to all speakers so that we can all ensure a productive event for everyone involved.

1. Please review, sign, and return the speaker consent form attached to this letter. This form must be completed, signed, and returned to us BEFORE you will be allowed to speak at the event. We suggest taking a moment to take care of the consent form now so that it does not become an issue later.

2. Please cater your information and presentation materials to our audience, which is small business owners and entrepreneurs. We also ask that you use information attendees can use and implement right away upon leaving the event. In other words, please tell them how to do it rather than what they need to do.

3. Please reserve the last 10 minutes of the time you have been allotted for Q&A.

4. We require you to speak with a microphone, which will be provided to you at the event. When conducting the Q&A portion of your presentation, we will also make a microphone available to audience members to ask questions.

5. We will be recording all of the sessions. Please be cognizant of the audiovisual professional that will be situated at the back of the room. This person will indicate any problems to you, or if they need you to pause for DVD or tape changes.

6. Please provide us with clean and professional copies of your handout materials. We will make copies for you to hand out during your sessions. We also will use these copies to make copies for individuals that purchase the home study course. These presentation materials are a great way to promote yourself and your business, so make sure your professionalism is shining through these materials.

7. Please get in the right mindset — a flexible mindset. Sometimes, we have to make time slot adjustments, room changes, or other unforeseen changes. We only do this when it is absolutely necessary, but we ask that you work with us and cooperate with us to make these changes as seamless as possible.

8. Please be present at the event even when you are not speaking. Participants and attendees will have questions for you. It behooves you to be available to answer these questions as much as it helps attendees get the answers to the questions that they have.

9. If you have products or service packages, feel free to pitch and sell them at the event. We also can provide you with an exhibit table on the showroom floor to sell during trade show hours. Please contact our office to make these arrangements.

Thank you again for speaking at our upcoming event. We know you will be a valuable addition to the lineup, and we know you and your business will benefit from the exposure as well. In the meantime, if you have any questions or concerns, please do not hesitate to contact us.

Sincerely,

Jane D. Doe

Jane D. Doe

Working with speakers

Once the speakers are on your agenda, remain in contact with them in the time leading up to the event. The speaker provides you with a copy of his or her presentation and speech ahead of time. This permits you to review the information they plan to share to ensure everything you need is in the lesson or speech.

If you are arranging travel and accommodations for the speakers, you or a staff member needs to work with them to make these arrangements. If the speaker is booking his or her own travel and hotel accommodations, you still need to be in contact with the speaker to obtain this information. Have your speakers fax or email you copies of their travel agendas so you know where they are every step of the way.

As speakers and educators arrive at the venue, have staff available to greet them. This leaves a good impression on your speakers and allows you to know when speakers arrive and if there are any problems in their arrival that might impede their speeches or sessions.

Have a speaker liaison available to your speakers throughout the seminars and workshops. This is especially true if you have a multiple-day event planned. The speakers need to have one point of contact they can turn to for any of their needs that might come up during the event. Keep your speakers as happy as possible.

As the event ends, also conduct a survey with your speakers, lecturers, educators, and experts who helped you implement the sessions. These professionals can provide you with valuable feedback on the good and not so good parts of the event. Especially those professionals who have experience speaking at other events can give you suggestions and alternative ways of doing things that you might not otherwise have thought of on your own.

As you start to research speakers and book them, you will also have a better idea of how much staffing your event is going to cost you. *In Chapter 5, you will uncover some of the other sources of money you have besides digging into your own pocket or the organization budget.*

Chapter Five

Funding, Sponsors, and Donations

Once you have a budget in place and know what items you require, then you can take a hard look at where to get the money to pay for these expenses. You already might have a budget for these events. If not, or to offset these costs, consider the various funding sources you have available. Additionally, learn how to obtain sponsors and donations for the items and services you need to pull the event together.

Evaluate Your Cash Sources

Once the budget is in place and you have a pretty good handle on what each item and service is going to cost you, it is then time to evaluate where you are going to get the money. Seminar and workshop hosts have three primary sources of funding for the event: the marketing budget for the business or organization, cash savings, and other cash sources. This section briefly will discuss the first two and the most obvious sources of funding. The remainder of the chapter, however, focuses on the alternative sources you can turn to as a means to drumming up additional cash, products, and even services you need for the event.

Marketing budget

If you are hosting the event for a business, association, or organization, these types of entities allocate a portion of their annual marketing budget for hosting events. If you are the business owner or professional responsible for coming up with the money, look into your own budget to determine where you can pull this money from, if you do not already have funds allocated.

Cash savings

When you do not have a line item in your marketing budget for events, start searching for pockets of cash you can pull from. Start by looking at any cash savings you have. Second, turn to the miscellaneous line items in your budget. You might not be able to cover the  expenses of the whole event from one source, but if you add a line item here and there, you just might scrape up enough cash to cover the costs.

Other cash sources

Other cash sources, however, can help you offset the amount of money you have to pay out of your own marketing budget or your own pocket. The two primary alternative sources of cash are sponsors and donors, which vary with each event. But keep reading because the rest of this chapter focuses on how you can establish sponsorship and donor programs that could conceivably cover the entire cost of your event, or at the least, cover the gap in expenses.

CASE STUDY: FUNDING THE INNOVATIVE WAY

OPIS Network
Norm Bour
4000 MacArthur Blvd 9th Floor
Newport Beach, CA 92660
(949) 495-6162
www.OPISNetwork.com
www.help100days.com

OPIS Networks is a business consultancy firm that creates competitive positioning through a series of 100MAD Days, which are 13-week programs designed to shift mindset radically and create improvement in business. Competitive positioning is also and one of the things the experts of the firm teach.

The first "helping 100 businesses for 100 days" rolled out in January 2010 with the city of Santa Ana, the eighth largest city in California. With the support of the mayor and city council, the event drew 200 attendees, and all of the comments were positive. The city asked OPIS Network to host three additional events. This event also opened the doors for other cities to follow, landed great media coverage, and genuinely provided goodwill for OPIS Network and its partners.

Partnering with nonprofits and Community Based Organizations (CBO) also has proved successful in the marketing and promotion arena. These types of organizations have members, followers, and a database. The organizations send out invitations and help to promote the event in exchange for exposure and a free table at the event for the organization.

Seminars, lunch and learns, and peer-to-peer classes have been integral to the business for years. To get greater exposure, OPIS Network created and customized programs for different chambers of commerce. The firm went a step further and taught the chambers as well as their members how to reinvent themselves. This program developed into several partnerships with cities throughout Southern California, and seven workshops with five different cities. OPIS Network is now finalizing a partnership with a major university to create regional programs, rather than specific to a city.

OPIS Network, like most companies, runs on a very lean philosophy. Since they partner with larger entities, OPIS Network asks their partners to cover the costs for the venue, food, some marketing, and some of the other costs for hosting the event. The return on investment (ROI) from workshops and seminars can be considerable, but so can the costs. Conducting a workshop must be very specific and the mechanics of closing the sale is an art as well as a science. Many free or inexpensive venues are available, which helps to lower the food or drink costs.

The purpose of using seminars and workshops is three-fold. First, it is a way to engage the audience with the insight that they must reinvent themselves to survive and thrive in today's world. Education is the key component of the event, as well as guiding audience member to reach their own conclusions. Second, OPIS Network uses these events as a platform for encouraging attendees to use the free workbook they provide so attendees can evaluate their business objectively. While OPIS Network is not big on "back of the room" sales, they do encourage attendees to join their 100-day program, which they use as an entry to move them closer to becoming a client.

Setting measurable goals comes to the bottom line, which are the sales OPIS Network generates from the event. They also evaluate how many attendees show up compared to how many were invited and how many registered to attend but did not attend. According to OPIS Network's Norm Bour, the company uses workshops and seminars to put "butts in seats, to be very direct." People do not tend to buy unless there is a relationship created and that involves either face-to-face or a very strong sales or online presence. Seminars and workshops allow the consultants to position themselves as experts, which makes the sales conversion much faster and easier than other forms of marketing.

Finding Sponsors

Sponsors are companies, businesses, organizations, foundations, associations, and individuals that have a stake in the event you are hosting. When one of these entities sponsors your event, it is a give-and-take relationship. The sponsor gives you cash, products in kind, or services in kind in return for marketing, public relations, and other benefits the entity receives from your event.

For example, a wedding vendor member association might sponsor a local bridal show. As part of its sponsorship, the association gives the bridal show planner $1,000 in cash and covers the cost of printing the agendas handed out to attendees as they enter the show. In return, you give the association logo placement and a mention of the association on all the marketing materials for the show. This includes all the marketing collateral that promotes the show leading up to the show date. It also includes banners, signs, and collateral handed out and any collateral from the show host that goes out to attendees.

In the same genre, a linen company might sponsor all the linens for the day of the event. They donate the use of table covers, chair covers, and decorations of this nature. This is product in-kind sponsorship. In return, the linen company receives a complimentary vendor table at the show, logo placement, and a mention in all the marketing collateral for the show.

Create sponsorship packages

Your first step in landing sponsors is to create sponsorship packages to illustrate the benefits they will get in return for sponsoring your event. A good rule is to create three sponsorship levels, which allows you a low-level, mid-level, and high-level package. To create an exclusivity feature for the sponsorship options, you might want to promote the packages so that you

have a limit on the number of sponsorships you will sell. This ensures sponsors, especially those at the highest level, and with the most benefits of sponsorship, they are not going to be clumped in with 50 other businesses, but rather an elite few.

Sticking with the bridal show sponsorships, here are some examples of the benefits the show planner might include in its sponsorship levels:

Diamond Level (Highest) $10,000

- Logo placement on all print marketing material
- Mention in all marketing collateral, speeches, and introductions
- Complimentary membership to the organization hosting the event/ professional organization associated with the group hosting the event
- Complimentary vendor table at the event
- Lunch for two representatives of the company/group
- Logo placement on website for the event
- Logo placement on main banner at entrance of event
- Two complimentary tickets to the award ceremony dinner
- Video placement about the company/association in the passage hallways during the event

Platinum Level (Middle) $5,000

- Logo placement on all print marketing material
- Mention in all marketing collateral, speeches, and introductions
- Complimentary membership to the organization hosting the event/ professional organization associated with the group hosting the event
- Complimentary vendor table at the event
- Logo placement on website for the event

Gold Level (Lowest) $2,500

- Logo placement on all print marketing material
- Mention in all marketing collateral, speeches, and introductions
- Complimentary vendor table at the event

You can get creative in naming your sponsorship levels, if you choose. Some event hosts name the sponsorship levels in terms that somehow relate to the industry. For example, the above packages relate to the wedding industry with the names diamond, platinum, and gold. For a convention for professional chefs, you could have names associated with foods or levels of chefs, such as King of the Kitchen, Sous Chef, and Baker. For a convention of scientists, you could use atomic elements to illustrate the different levels of sponsorship. Have fun with this, and be as creative as possible.

Once you create the names or three levels, it is time to start filling in what the sponsor gives you and what the sponsor receives from sponsoring your event. The higher the sponsorship level, the more benefits you must include.

The dollar amounts next to the levels are up to you to determine. If someone is giving you $10,000, for example, your benefits should amount to $10,000 worth. Remember, the sponsors might give you $10,000 in cash or they might give you $10,000 worth of products or services.

Contact and book sponsors

After you have created your sponsorship packages, the next step is to determine viable sponsors for your event. Create a list of all potential sponsors you can think of for the event. After you compile the list, which is going to be your target list — the list of entities you are going to contact — compile all the contact information. You even might want to take it a step further and research the other types of events these entities have sponsored. If they have sponsored events similar to your event in the past, then you have a better chance of getting them to sponsor your event than if they do not sponsor events or they sponsor events of a different nature.

With the target list in hand, decide the types of contact you want to employ. For example, you might start by making a phone call first. In some circumstances, the person responsible for making these decisions will talk to you and agree to sponsor the event. In other circumstances, they will request additional information.

For those who agree to sponsor the event on the spot, go over the sponsorship packages with them. When they choose their level of sponsorship, send a sponsorship agreement. This does not have to be a complicated legal document. It can just state that your entity and their entity agree to the following terms and conditions. Spell out what you are providing to them and what they are providing to you. Both parties should sign it and date it.

If target sponsors request additional information, send them a sponsorship cover letter, sponsorship package sheet, and a description of the event you are hosting. You can print this on your company letterhead or the letterhead you create for the event itself. You might want to include a sponsorship agreement in the package, so if they decide to sponsor the event, they have everything they need. In most cases, you will need to follow up with the potential sponsors that request additional information.

For the entities you cannot contact via phone, you might wish to assemble a letter to mail or an email to send. If you sent an informational packet to target sponsors, you can use a version of that cover letter. You can find a sample sponsorship cover letter in the Appendix.

You also will have target sponsors that turn you down. If you get a no, you can say thank you and hang up, or you can ask if they might be interested in making a donation instead. Again, you might get a no, or you might receive a cash donation that helps to offset any expenses for the event that you do not have the money to pay for at the moment.

Ask for Donations

Donations are just that — cash donations that companies, businesses, associations, organizations, or individuals make without any benefits in return. People make donations to help benefit the recipient of the donation amount but do not expect anything in return. The goal in making a donation is to help the purpose of the event, so you will receive donations from those who believe there is a need for the type of event you are hosting. Donations can take the form of services, goods, or straight cash. In the case of donations, however, the most popular form is cash. People donate, and then their obligation is complete.

Service donations

The first type of donation is a service. An individual or company might donate its services to your event. In return, you do not have to provide anything to them. In other words, a donation is different from a sponsorship relationship because the donor is not receiving anything from you in return.

An example of a service donation would be if the venue where you are hosting the event throws in all the wait staff and bartenders at no extra cost to you. Although they might charge you to rent the space and the food and beverages, they might be willing to donate the service providers.

Goods donations

The second type of donation is a product. An individual or company might donate its products to your event. You do not have to provide anything to them for a good donation, either.

Goods for the event can be anything you need or want for your event. It might be the venue, catering, audiovisual equipment, linens, printing, swag bags, or anything else you could possibly need to host the event.

Cash donations

The final, and most popular, donation is a cash donation. The donor writes you a check, gives you a money order, or hands you cash. You can add this cash to the amount you have to cover the expenses of the event. You can use this cash for anything you want as long as it pertains to the event for which the donor gave you the money.

Most events use some combination of its own money, sponsorships, and donations to cover all its expenses. If you have the cash to host your event and do not wish to get involved with sponsors and donors, then this is fine as well. Some event hosts are forced to turn to sponsors and donors because they do not have enough cash in their marketing budget to pull the event off or to pull it off at a beneficial level.

The rest of your journey in planning the event focuses in on the day of the event — the delivery. *Chapter 6 delves into all the aspects you need to focus on to prepare for the big debut.*

Chapter Six

Get Ready to Deliver

In Chapter 6, you will learn the steps to prepare for the big day. This includes putting together the informational packets and handouts and preparing the audiovisual elements of your presentation. It also will guide you on how to plan room setups and flow charts for transition from each room. Additionally, it will walk you through turning your preliminary agenda into its final stage. The chapter includes a venue checklist and day-before checklist to ensure you have everything you need to set up and implement the event.

Room Setups

Contact the coordinator for the venue where you are hosting the event. Most hotels and venues for rent can provide you with floor plans. The floor plans should include all areas you are using for your event. Use the copies of the floor plans and a pencil to draw in and plan the placement of everything. Do this with each room you have. You can share copies of these diagrams with the vendors, the venue, staff, and anyone else who needs to know where things are supposed to go.

Use a pencil because you might need to change and rearrange as the day of the event approaches. It is a good idea to learn how to draw to scale, and make sure the floor plan is to scale, so you know if the setup you choose fits into the space you have. Even if you do not plan to scale, you can draw in the setup, but you might have to make adjustments according to the space in the room.

When you are drawing the setup onto the floor plans, include everything. Make sure the diagram includes:

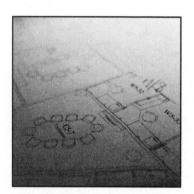

- Stage/platform for speaker

- Chalkboard, whiteboard, easel for speaker

- Projection screen

- TV, projectors, laptop table

- Tables for attendees

- Chairs for attendees

- Refreshment tables

- Product or marketing collateral table

- Podium

Agenda

When it comes to creating an agenda for the event, you have to create two versions. The primary agenda is what you will hand out to the attendees. In addition to this portion of the agenda, you will need to add setup and teardown information for the staff and vendors, as well as any information that relates specifically to the staff and vendors. You can find sample agendas for guests and staff in the Appendix.

For example, the agenda for the attendees contains only the information that pertains to them, such as the specific breakout sessions and social events they preregistered to attend. The agenda for the staff would include the same information as it does for attendees but would also include what time the staff needs to arrive for setup on the day before the event, when the lunch break room is setup for them to eat, and what the hours are for the breakdown of the event rooms when the event is over.

Type the agenda up in a word processing or spreadsheet program. This makes it faster and easier to make changes than writing it out on paper. Additionally, you can print or have these agendas printed on the correct paper without having to have the printer typeset and format the agenda.

Both types of agendas are key components to the event. You should include the staff and vendor agenda in the informational packets. The agenda for attendees can go on the event website or page and in information packets that go out to attendees before the event, and a final version of the agenda can be handed to attendees when they check in to the event.

Informational Packets and Handouts

Although the agenda is one of the pieces that go into the informational packets, several other pieces also tend to make up informational packets. You want informational packets for attendees, but you also should have informational packets for the event staff, vendors, and speakers. There will be some overlap in the information each of these packets contains. Some of the information you will have to create from scratch so that it is applicable to the group receiving the packets.

Some of the information included in staff informational packets includes:

- Setup time

- Break times

- Whether refreshments are provided or they need to take care of their own needs

- Dress code

- Name badge

- Floor plan copies

- Description of the specific role they are to play leading up, on the day of, and after the event

Some of the information included in speaker informational packets includes:

- Travel information/itinerary with transportation, and hotel

- Speaking times and places/rooms

- Whether refreshments are provided or they need to take care of their own needs

- Suggested dress code

- Name badge

- Floor plan copies

- Tickets to social events or admission to other aspects of the event

Some of the information included in attendee informational packets includes:

- Travel information/itinerary with transportation, and hotel

- Event agenda

- Floor plan listing where each vendor is located, where the workshop is taking place, and where break rooms and social areas are

- Marketing information vendors, sponsors, or donors want to include

- Name tag

- Tickets to social events or admission to other aspects of the event

- Surveys for each speaker, lecturer, and expert registered to speak

You also might need to assemble or create any handouts the attendees need for the event. Some speakers, lecturers, and experts might provide you with information they want attendees to take away from the sessions. If they do, you might choose to make copies of this information and include it in the information packets you send to attendees, or you might choose to provide these packets when they check in to the event.

Handouts might be the feedback questionnaires or surveys you give attendees. Anything that you can prepare or acquire ahead of time helps cut down on the time you have to spend rushing around in the days leading up to the event. You will have plenty to keep you busy, so focus on getting anything you possibly can out of the way.

CASE STUDY: PREPARE TO DELIVER

Expanding Thought Inc.©
Marian Thier
3180 Westwood Court
Boulder, Colorado
(303) 440-1278
www.xtho.com and www.
listeningimpact.com

Expanding Thought Inc. is a coaching, training, consulting, and assessment provider company. Owner Marian Thier also speaks at conferences and at companies on how the brain, body, and emotions create listening habits that form human interactions. As part of the company's business plan, they conduct webinars, seminars, and workshops for clients on a broad range of leadership, creativity, innovation, and communication practices.

Because Expanding Thought Inc. does not offer public workshops; it custom focuses each event for client needs. In most cases, Thier or one of her staff, speaks with someone from the client organization to identify their issues, population, requirements, and outcomes. Once they know the population and the context, then they are able to custom build a program. Most of the programs include a workshop or webinar, assessments, and coaching. They rarely do a workshop that does not include additional consulting and/or coaching after the event is over.

After preparing the information and customizing the workshop to fit the client's needs, Thier says it is just as important to practice the delivery of the information before the day of the event. The first step she takes in preparing is to review the workshop flow "to make sure I know the content and timing." This allows her to pinpoint any areas where she might need more information. If so, she conducts research on any concepts that may need further exploration or to explore the most recent findings. She then annotates the workshop design for key points, and if a PowerPoint presentation is part of the workshop, Thier notates timing and notes for each slide. She reduces everything to a one color-coded page or a few index cards. Her color-coding system assigns a different color to each aspect of the presentation, such as timing, key points, questions, and transition. Finally, she rehearses until she is confident she can deliver the workshop without any notes.

Thier also prepares her supplemental materials for each workshop. She always uses materials that incorporate the different thinking styles, informed by the Herrmann Brain Dominance Instrument® (HBDI®). For example, when her group composition is younger people, she uses video, written handouts, and interactive games to reinforce the learning and comprehension of the information she is sharing.

Thier does not use workbooks in her workshops and seminars. Instead, she has participants use a capture journal that is a double-sided tri-fold. All key concepts and their thoughts are included in the capture journal. The purpose is for participants to have a take-away that they will actually use.

Name Tags

Your guests, staff, speakers, and other personnel need name tags. If speakers and attendees have their own name tags, encourage them to bring them and wear them at the event. If you represent a membership organization that has professional name tags or name tags of any kind that you pass out and collect at each meeting, have these name tags ready for the event. Match the list of attendees and speakers with the name badges you already have, and put them on order far in advance.

If you professionally produce or print name tags ahead of time, you can place these badges on a table in alphabetical order for pickup on arrival at the event. You also might choose to include the name badge inside the information packet the attendees pick up when they check into the event. Even if you print badges ahead of time, you will miss people or others that show up on the day of the event. Be sure to have extra name badges and writing utensils for these people to create a name badge on the spot.

If you do not want to print name tags ahead of time, you also have the option to provide name tags and writing utensils for the day of the event. These types of name badges are best left to one-day events because once you peel off the name tag, it is useless.

You also have the option to use name badges. Attendees can still write their own names on the tag. The tag then slides into a plastic cover with a clip or lanyard. This type of name badge can be created on the spot and used multiple times for a multiple-day event.

Audiovisual

Your audiovisual needs vary with each event. The bigger an event is, the more types of audiovisual equipment are required. A small event, or a one-room event, might not require any audiovisual equipment. In the following sections, you will find some of the more prominent needs when it comes to hosting an event and the audiovisual equipment needed. *Revisit Chapter 4 for more information about hiring vendors.*

Speakers' needs

The best way to start evaluating your audiovisual needs is to speak with your speakers, lecturers, and experts. Find out their needs. Find out what they are bringing with them versus what you need to supply. Some speakers have their own wireless microphone or headset microphone. In this case, you do not need to provide this, but you will need to provide speakers and an amplifier that is compatible with the mic they are using.

Speakers might have slides on their laptop, so they will bring their laptop loaded with the presentation it. You will need to provide the projector and the screen for them to use to project their presentation. After you have the needs of your experts compiled, then you can start evaluating the audiovisual needs for the other areas of the event.

Microphones

Especially for events with large rooms, one or more microphones are a standard requirement. Even if it is a small room but you or your speaker is not someone who can project his or her voice, consider using a microphone during your seminar or workshop. You can rent microphones through the hotel or venue. Otherwise, you will need to contact an audiovisual company that rents out this type of equipment.

Speakers

If you are playing music at your event or are using a microphone, you are also going to need speakers. Some venues have a speaker system installed in the rooms, so it is a matter of hooking the microphone up to the speakers. If the venue does not have its own speakers and other audio equipment, you will have to rent from an audiovisual provider.

Amplifiers

For large rooms, you might need an amplifier in addition to the speakers and microphone. The amplifier increases the sound production from the speakers and the microphone. Amplifiers either are provided by the venue or you have to rent them, as is the case with speakers and microphones. Amplifiers come in different sizes, so discuss the room size and the number of attendees with the audiovisual company or venue. The audiovisual professional can work with you to provide the right size amplifier you need to project the sound adequately in the space you have available. Although you will need to sketch the equipment into your room diagram, the audiovisual staff or the venue staff sets up the equipment, not the event planner.

Screens

You might need a screen for projecting a presentation onto the wall from a laptop computer. You also might need a projection screen if you are showing any movies, commercials, or other types of videos. Some venues have screens built into the rooms you rent. If these screens do not exist, rent portable screens that can be brought in for the day and removed when the event is over.

Projectors

When you are discussing your audiovisual needs with your venue and with the speakers and lecturers, include projectors into your plan. If a speaker is using PowerPoint, showing a DVD, or has another need for projecting information on the screen, you will need a projection machine. If the venue where the event is being held does not have a projector, contact an audiovisual company that can provide a rental machine and possibly someone to set it up for you.

DVD player and TVs

Many events use DVDs that operate on a loop. Hotels and conference centers make DVDs and TVs readily available as part of their menu of services. If not, you can rent the items, or even bring in a player and TV of your own.

Extension cords

With all this electronic equipment, another major item to add to your list of required items is extension cords. Because most outlets only have two plugs, it is likely you will need extension cords to create availability. Additionally, the extension cords permit you to place your electronic equipment where it needs to go, even if it is not close to a wall or floor outlet.

Informational Packets for Speakers/Educators

One of the most important pieces to put together for the day of your event is the informational packet you hand out to your speakers, lecturers, and educators. The information these packets contain is valuable to the people who are front and center at your event. These are the packets the speakers receive when they check into their hotel for the event or when they check in on the day of the event. Although some of the information you include might vary, ensure that you include some essential components of the packet:

- **Event agenda** — First, provide an agenda for the entire event. If it is a one-day event, then this might be on one sheet. If it is a multiple-day event, include the schedule for each day of the event. This provides the educator with a big-picture view of everything taking place.

- **Teaching schedule** — The next thing you want to include in the informational packet is the personalized schedule for the educator. Because it is customized, this portion of the packet requires you to create a unique agenda for each person speaking at the event. On this sheet, include the dates and times of where the speakers need to be for their presentations. Include setup times, arrival times, start times, and end times so the speaker knows precisely how the event is to unfold. You also should include the name or room number where they are speaking.

- **Event map** — Include a floor plan, map, or layout of the event. In one glance, the map should provide the speaker with an idea of where important locations are in the building. Highlight the room or rooms where the speaker will be presenting, so it is easy for them to identify where they are then and where they need to be for their presentation.

- **Name tag** — If you are providing name tags for the speakers, also slide this into the information packet. If your budget permits, you might want to include two name tags. This provides a backup in case they lose or misplace the original name tag. This is not a necessity, but rather a nicety.

- **Admission tickets** — If the event is hosting any special social events that require admission tickets, the information packet is the perfect place to provide these to your speakers. Clearly label the admission tickets so that the speaker knows which event the ticket is for, the date and time of the special event, and the location of the event.

- **Contact sheet** — It is a good idea to include a one-page important contacts information sheet in the speaker's informational packets as well. This sheet includes the contact name, phone number, cell phone number, email address, and any other pertinent contact information the speaker might require. Clearly label what role the person plays or for which reasons the speaker might need to contact the person. For example, if the speaker is having an audiovisual problem with his or her equipment, then he or she will need to contact the hotel resort where the event is taking place. If the speaker needs copies made because he or she is running low on handouts, then he or she should contact the administrative assistant in the business center.

- **Area map** — Contact the chamber of commerce or tourist information center for the town or city in which you are hosting the event. They can offer you area maps to include in the information packets. In their downtime, or if the speakers choose to arrive early or add days onto their stays, they have maps of the area to see what gems the town or city holds.

- **Area transportation information** — Provide a sheet of information on the transportation options for the area, so speakers know how to get around town. Taxis, buses, a hotel shuttle, or rental car services that service the area are options to think about including on the sheet.

- **Amenities and Activities** — You can handle the amenities and activities information in different ways. One way is to compile on one or two sheets a list of the activities in the area. You can write a small, one paragraph description of the activity and include the address, phone number, and website for the location of the activity. If you live or work in the town or city where you are hosting the event, you likely can list these activities off the top of your head and research the contact information. A second way to handle this is to gather brochures or information sheets from the locations or from the local tourism bureau. Slide the individual brochures or information sheets into the packet.

- **Survey** — The speaker information packets are also a good way to distribute the survey questionnaire you want your speakers to complete and submit. Include submission information on the survey so that speakers know what to do with the surveys when they complete it.

Speaker information packets are compiled in a one- or two-pocket folder. If you use a one-pocket folder, place the items in order of use. If you use a two-pocket folder, place the information that directly pertains to the event in the right pocket and extraneous information in the left pocket.

Venue Checklist

A valuable tool to create for your event is a series of checklists for your venue. Having these checklists prepared before the event helps to ensure that everything from setup to tear down is taken care of and that no important details are overlooked. The two primary checklists for the venue are the day before checklist and the day of checklist.

Day before checklist

For bigger events, especially ones with multiple rooms to set up, you are likely to set up the event rooms at least one day before the event. You want to go into the event venue after the venue staff or hired staff has completed the room setup with your checklist in hand. Use the checklist and go to each area and room to verify that everything you need is there and where it should be.

Confirm setup is correct

Create a setup checklist for each room or area of the event. For example, have a checklist available for the information area, the check-in area, the main ballroom where the keynote speaker is, and each of the session breakout rooms.

Checklist items should include:

- **Tables and chairs** — Check that the type of tables, number of tables, and the placement of the tables are correct. Conduct the same check for the chairs.

- **Linens** — Check that the table and chair linens are on the tables and chairs. Color options also should be verified then.

- **Room setup** — Compare the room diagram to the actual room setup. Place a checkmark on your diagram as you confirm that the item is in the room and in the place it should be.

- **Test audiovisual equipment** — Confirm that all the audiovisual equipment is plugged in and hooked up correctly. Turn all the equipment on and test it to make sure it is working.

Confirm room/rooms are set up

Use the floor plan of the event to confirm that all the rooms and areas you requested exist. Use the flow of traffic that your attendees and behind-the-scenes staff will use. Start at the front entrance of the venue. Walk up to the check-in area. You have used the checklists in the previous section to confirm the setup for each of these areas is correct. This exercise simply helps to confirm that all the areas and rooms are ready to go.

Using your diagram, move on from the check-in area to the next area on your map. After you verify each room or area setup, place a checkmark on your diagram so that you know you can move on to the next area. Continue to do this until you have confirmed all the areas on your floor plan or map.

Confirm arrival and check-in of speakers

Unless the speakers are local, you also want to confirm that your speakers have arrived and checked into their hotels the day before the event. This might require you to send a quick email or make a phone call to each speaker or lecturer to confirm his or her arrival. If you have the speakers check in with one of your staff on their arrival and the staff member hands over the speaker information packet, then you should have a one-sheet checklist that shows in one glance which speakers have arrived and which still might be coming. For any last-minute stragglers, have a plan in place to confirm their arrival.

Avoid finding out that one of your speakers or lecturers has not arrived in town on the day of the event. You will, however, conduct a second check-in confirmation

on the day of checklist to confirm that the speakers and lecturers are on site and in place for the event to start.

Schedule practice for speakers

Another item to consider for your checklist is practice for the speakers or lecturers. After you have gone through the venue and everything is in place and ready to roll, have the speakers and lecturers run through a practice exercise. Have them hook up their presentations or use any technical equipment they need for the speech to make sure you can work out any bugs or glitches before show time.

Scheduling practice allows you and the speakers to pinpoint any current or potential problems. Hosting a practice before the opening day of the event helps limit the issues that might arise on the day of the event and during each presentation.

It is also a good idea to pack a small kit of supplies. As the seminar or workshop host, you might want to keep some general items on hand. These supplies come in handy for quick fixes and to prevent minor malfunctions from becoming major issues. You can use this checklist as a guide and modify it as necessary as you encounter new situations.

Extra blank name tags
Pens
Chalk/markers for erase board
Masking tape
Registration sheets
Timer/stopwatch
Cash/change for sales
Receipt book
Credit card processor
Stapler
Staples
Scissors

Paper tablets

Straight pins

Thumbtacks

Registrant list

Handouts

Notes for presentation

Props

Presentation/overhead slides

Audio/video recorder

Blank audio and video CDs/DVDs

DVDs, videos and training materials

Vendor contact list

Products to sell

Information on future events

Promotion materials

Business cards

Brochures

Sales sheets

Evaluations/questionnaires

Day of checklist

Starting with a walk through the day before
the event ensures that everything is as final as it
can be before you open the doors to attendees.
Even if only a few hours pass between your
check the day before and the final check you
are about to conduct with information from
this section, it is good practice to run the final
check to make sure all the final details are taken
care of and your event is ready to roll.

In a way, the day of checklist is a second check of the event, equipment, speakers,
and all the other details that went into planning the seminar or workshop.

First, repeat the checklist you used the day before:

Checklist items should include:

- **Tables and chairs** — Check that the type of tables, number of tables,
  and the placement of the tables are correct. Conduct the same check for
  the chairs.

- **Linens** — Check that the table and chair linens are on the tables and
  chairs. Color options also should be verified then.

- **Room setup** — Compare the room diagram to the actual room setup.
  Place a checkmark on your diagram as you confirm that the item is in the
  room and in the place it should be.

- **Test audiovisual equipment** — Confirm that all the audiovisual
  equipment is plugged in and hooked up correctly. Turn all the equipment
  on, and test it to make sure it is working.

The day of the event, also confirm that everything with the food and beverage setup is correct. Even if the tables that hold the food and beverages were set up on your day-before check, now you need to confirm that the food and drinks you ordered have arrived as promised. Additionally, check for any items necessary to consume the food, such as:

- Cups/glasses

- Plates

- Bowls

- Silverware (forks, knives, and spoons)

- Napkins (paper or linen)

- Condiments (sugar, sweeteners, milk/creamer, ketchup, mustard, and mayonnaise)

- Straws/drink stirrers

- Serving utensils (tongs, spoons, and forks)

Confirm arrival of speakers at location

Have a system in place to confirm that the speakers are on site and ready to go. The easiest way to handle this is to have a check-in station manned with a staff member. Have the speakers check in so that you have an up-to-date list of the speakers that are present and accounted for. About 30 minutes before the doors open to attendees, do a walk through to ensure that each speaker is in his or her room, set up, and ready to start the presentation. This also provides you with the opportunity to do a last-minute check to make sure the speakers have everything they need and are not experiencing any technical difficulties.

If for some reason speakers are not in their rooms or have not checked in, this last-minute check gives you some time to locate the speaker. In extreme circumstances, if you cannot locate the speaker and the speaker is not present, then you also have time to go to "Plan B." Plan B is to put another speaker in the place of the missing speaker or rearrange where attendees of the session go for the current time slot.

Check staff members are in place

Another imperative check is to make sure that the people staffing the various tables and stations throughout the venue are in place and ready to fulfill their roles. Staff members, volunteers, and employees should be in place at least 30 minutes before the start time of the event. This ensures that as speakers, other staff members, and attendees arrive, everyone is in place and ready to help make the event as successful as possible.

Once you have done your final walk-through of the venue and everything is in place, it is time to open the doors to attendees. Get ready, take a deep breath, and prepare yourself because once those doors open, it tends to be a busy day.

All your hard work is for naught if attendees do not register for the seminars and workshops you are hosting. *In Chapter 7, you will uncover online and offline marketing techniques to reach ideal attendees and motivate them to register for your event.*

Chapter Seven

Marketing the Seminar & Workshop to the Right Audience

You might have the best seminar or workshop topic chosen, but if nobody attends, then all your hard work is for naught. Chapter 7 helps you unravel exactly who your target audience is — the consumers, professionals, or groups that will benefit from the  information and knowledge you are sharing. The first step in marketing the seminar is to know precisely whom the audience is that you are trying to attract. The chapter also covers the online and offline marketing efforts, techniques, and tactics to draw the audience to your seminars and workshops.

Identify Your Target Audience

The first step in successfully marketing your seminars and workshops is to identify your target audience. The target audience includes all potential attendees that can benefit from the information, products, and services you are offering. You can break your target audience down into three primary groups: consumers, professionals, and groups. Depending on the topics you are covering with your workshops and seminars, you might have potential attendees in all three categories, or you only might have prospects that fall into one or two categories.

In the next three sections, you will find information on the types of attendees that might fall into the three broad categories. Study each one carefully. As you read the descriptions, start to think about any attendees that might fall into this category for the seminar or workshop you are currently planning.

Consumers

Consumers are individuals who have an interest in the topics you are covering at your event. Individuals might fall into demographic categories by gender, age, or interests. For example, a personal coach who works with women that are transitioning from a professional to a stay-at-home mom might identify the target audience as women between the ages of 25 and 45 at a management to an executive management position (currently working or recently left the business world) and currently has one or more children.

A college preparation company, on the other hand, might target households in the Anaheim, California, area that has children who are juniors in high school. Additionally, this type of company might target households with minimum household incomes of $150,000.

Professionals

Another broad category to consider is professional affiliations. Primarily, you are concerned with the profession of the prospective attendees when your target market is the business world or when you are an educator for specific industries or professions. For example, if you are hosting an annual conference as a human resource association, then your target audience might be employees that work in the human resource department of medium- to large-size companies in the United States.

A business attorney might specialize in providing legal advice and handling legal matters for small business owners involved in accounting services. This attorney might host a seminar on a topic or topics that relate directly to these types of professionals. He or she might set parameters, such as a revenue range that the business has on an annual basis and that the accounting company business owners are certified public accountants (CPAs).

Groups that will benefit from the information and knowledge you are sharing

Especially in situations of an educational or industry-focused nature, the third primary category is groups. If you are a scientific research organization, your target audience specifically might be the members of the association for which you are hosting the event. A nanny service might be targeting mommy-and-me groups in the Miami-metro area. The topic might be activities to stimulate the minds of your babies while spending quality time with your children.

After you identify the broad categories of possible attendees, then start to narrow your focus down to subcategories that fall under each primary category.

CASE STUDY: IN ORDER
PLEASE: IDENTIFYING
YOUR TARGET AUDIENCE
AND EDUCATING THEM

Create New Order, Inc.
Jennifer Ryan
P.O. Box 899
Kings Park, NY 11754
(631) 979-9530
www.createneworder.com

Create New Order, Inc., provides commercial and residential organizing services. Some of the organizing services include attics, basements, garages, hoarding, retrofit homes due to disability, art installations, risk management, customer service training, quality control inspections, file systems, home offices, space efficiency, utilization design, and decorating. The company finds and implements organizing solutions for clients.

Jennifer Ryan, owner of Create New Order Inc., hosts anywhere from three to 24 seminars or workshops per year. These events are part of her business plan to create the visibility of the company and the services she provides, while providing education, relief, and humor to potential clients. Hosting workshops and seminars enables Ryan to reach specific demographics and market her services based on specific topics.

In 2008, when the economy was in a drastic decline, Ryan's mission was to increase workshops to maintain a steady stream of income when there was a huge possibility of the loss of individual clients. Because organizing services is a luxury service, loss of clients and loss of income was a potential problem for Ryan. Her workshops and seminars continued to be a great way to fill the audience with potential clients, and she was able to retain all of her existing clients, while gaining new clients — some of which came directly from the workshops.

Ryan and her staff go through a specific process to research and build the profile for the types of attendees that should come to the seminar or workshop. First, they choose a hot topic, something that is popular and trending. For example, the topic might be, "Organize to de-clutter that small space." From the topic, they develop a target audience, which in this case is occupants of "small spaces," such as apartment/co-op/condo dwellers. Then they begin to identify a venue based on an area with a high concentration of apartment/co-op/condo buildings. Once they identify the audience, then the staff conducts research to see which channels of marketing and advertising are the best ways to reach this particular audience. The informational seminars and workshops Ryan offers are free, which helps draw audiences.

Ryan hosts seminars and workshops as part of the business and marketing plan because her target audience is often overwhelmed and ashamed. The mere thought of having anyone witness their "stuff" firsthand is a traumatic thought, never mind taking action to organize their stuff. Ryan's talents for talking and providing information in an entertaining manner allow people to come and hear how their lives could improve through organization without them having to expose their clutter. With Ryan's energy and the information she provides, her audience experiences relief along with motivation and humor, allowing them to either take action on their own or look for the resources, such as the ones Create New Order, Inc., provides, to help them organize.

Marketing Your Event

To put your marketing plan into perspective, it is a good idea to create a written marketing plan. The marketing plan works as a guide for you to follow to make sure that you have a systemized plan in place to promote and market your event. Your marketing plan consists of all the potential attendees for the seminar or workshop you are hosting and indirectly could benefit from any products or services you might be selling at the event. It is a study of your target market: Who  is buying, why they are buying, and how you will surpass the competition and get that market to buy from you.

The following worksheet will help you put your thoughts down on paper. Completing the answers to the question will help you focus and organize your marketing efforts for maximum efficiency and effectiveness.

Marketing plan worksheet

Who are the potential attendees of the seminar(s) or workshop(s)? Who is most likely to benefit from the information and resources you are sharing at the event?

_____

_____

_____

_____

Who are your competitors? Who are the other professionals offering similar events? Who are the other groups or organizations that attract the same audience you are looking to target?

_____

_____

_____

_____

How can you compete in this market?

_____

_____

_____

_____

What are your strengths and weaknesses in comparison to competitors? What benefits do your seminars and workshops offer that your competitors do not?

_____

_____

_____

_____

What type of image do you want to portray for your event, products, and services?

_____

_____

_____

_____

What is your pricing strategy?

_____

_____

Is your pricing in line with your image?

_____

_____

Do your prices properly cover costs?

_____

_____

What types of promotions will you use (television, radio, direct mail, personal contacts, newspaper, magazines, Yellow Pages, billboards, Internet, classifieds, and trade associations)?

_____

_____

_____

_____

Once you have this worksheet complete, you have a guide to follow to work through marketing and promoting your event. The next two primary sections of the chapter cover the specific ways you can market and promote the event and attract attendees via online and offline methods. As you read these sections, go back and adjust your marketing plan worksheet to reflect any ideas gleaned from these sections.

Marketing Strategy

The marketing plan is the action part of promoting your seminars, workshops, and events. You can take these steps proactively to market the event, make people aware it exists, and find attendees to register. With the right mix of online and offline marketing tactics, you can attract attendees that fall into your target market.

One important factor to keep in mind is that marketing an event is a process. You cannot conduct a marketing activity one time and then decide that it is a complete failure because you do not see immediate results. You must take consistent action in implementing your marketing strategies for at least six months to a year before an event.

If you have a shorter lead time before your event, you still can use all these marketing tactics, but the volume you do needs to increase because you have a shorter lead time to make these efforts count. Additionally, those with an existing lead list can work on a shorter schedule, if necessary, because you already have potential attendees to market the event to while you are working to generate new leads.

The first part of the marketing plan is the marketing strategy, which is a three-step system. Commit these three strategies to memory because every marketing activity covered in the remainder of the plan hinges on them.

1. Gather qualified leads and followers to grow your subscriber list and database.

2. Nurture the qualified leads and followers in your database by consistently getting in front of them, in various ways, with information about your event.

3. Convert the leads into registrations.

CASE STUDY: WRITE TO SUCCEED: MARKETING & PROMOTING SUCCESSFUL SEMINARS ON A SHOESTRING BUDGET

Gloria Rand SEO Copywriter
Gloria Rand
1809 E. Broadway
Suite 302
Ovedo, FL 32765
(786) 942-8321
www.gloriarand.com

Gloria Rand provides SEO copywriting, blog writing, and social media consulting and training services to small businesses. Rand uses online seminars to generate leads for her copywriting business and to sell products and services, such as e-books and in-person training.

Ninety percent of Rand's seminars are online, which means low costs for marketing and promoting the events, as well as hosting the events. Besides her time, Rand only pays a monthly webinar service fee. Her marketing expenses are zero because she only advertises the seminar to her database of contacts and via social media networks, such as Facebook®, Twitter®, and LinkedIn®.

Since cost is not a factor, Rand rates her online seminar success rate by the number of registrants and the number of attendees. She aims for 100 registrants with a 30 to 40 percent attendance rate. With these numbers, Rand can typically convert about 10 percent of the registrants or attendees into new leads for her copywriting services. Rand says if she can hit these numbers, then she deems the seminar as a success.

While she does not focus too much of an effort or money on offline advertising, she did find one of the best ways to market the online seminars was from an article she wrote that was published in a networking group magazine. Rand finds that she achieves the best results from email marketing. She invites her list to attend the workshop. Approximately 80 to 90 percent of the attendees register from the email they receive. Her second biggest marketing tool is Facebook.

Rand says the best way to get started in hosting seminars and workshops is to attend seminars that others are hosting in your industry. This provides you with firsthand experience on what works and what does not work. You can emulate the good portions of the seminar and tweak the aspects of the event that did not work well. She also suggests you ask for questions from attendees before the day of the event. This permits you to answer these questions in case people are afraid to speak up when the time comes.

Marketing foundation

Before you can start to implement and integrate the various marketing activities, you first have to build your marketing foundation. Because the first half of the marketing plan covers the online activities you can partake in to attract attendees, the event Web page or website needs to be up and fully functioning so that you have a venue to drive traffic to when marketing the event.

Traffic should be driven to the website from a variety of venues, which will be discussed later in the plan. Driving traffic to the home page of the website will be an important first step to gathering leads and converting them into registrations. It will set the stage for learning more about these prospects and then converting them into registrations.

By incorporating certain elements into your Web design, you can increase the credibility of your event, which allows you to gather highly targeted leads that can be further qualified and turned into admission ticket sales. The following are elements your website should include:

Entice with an early-bird special — Offer an incentive to attendees who register by a specific date. An early-bird special might be a discount rate off the normal registration price. Right away, you are giving the visitors and prospective attendees a reason to sign up now — to get everything your event has to offer at a reduced rate. Another incentive might be some bonus items or events for anyone who registers before the early-bird special expires. For example, you might be hosting a cocktail reception on the second evening of the event. Normally, you would sell tickets to the event that are in addition to the registration fee. You might give a free admission ticket to the first 100 people that register for the event.

Registration form — If the visitor wants to register to attend the event, then have an online registration form. They can complete and submit this form online. You can work with your website designer to configure this form. If you are designing your own website, you can find form templates that can be personalized for your needs to add to the site.

You also need a payment processing system to collect the payment from the attendee. PayPal® is a free online option that provides payment buttons for your website. The website does deduct a percentage of the transaction as a fee for using its service. If you have a merchant account and offline payment processing system, then you simply can collect the payment information. You can run the payment manually offline.

You might want to offer a downloadable and printable registration option as well. This allows visitors to print and complete the registration form. They can mail the form in with a check or provide you with their credit card information.

Whether you provide online, offline, or both types of registration forms, ensure that the submission directions are clear. An online submission form requires a submission button on the website. A printed form should contain the mailing address where the form can be mailed.

See *Appendix E* for sample registration information.

Prospects that remain prospects — Although the above information pertains to visitors that come to the site and register, you also want to capture lead information on visitors who do not immediately register. Include a subscription box on your website, where at a minimum, you are capturing the name and email address for the visitor. This allows you to continue to communicate with potential attendees. This will allow you to implement step two of the strategy, which is to nurture the leads.

Further qualify attendees and subscriber leads — It is hard to get to know your attendees with just a registration form or to get to know subscribers to your list with just a name and an email address. As part of the subscription process, add a one-question survey to the registration form or the subscription. Use a question that directly relates to the challenges your target audience might face. For example, a staffing or human resource event form or subscription question might ask, "What is your biggest challenge or obstacle in landing the perfect employees?" The point of the question is to find out what your attendees and prospective attendees are thinking, feeling, or seeking information on from your event. You then can use the information you gather to ensure that these topics are covered at the event and even incorporate it into the marketing materials.

Optimize your pages — Use keywords in the copy of your website that prospective clients would use to search for the information your event is providing; this is the basis of search engine optimization (SEO). Choose one or two keywords to focus on for each page of your site, and then scatter the keywords, phrase, and combinations of the phrase in the beginning, in the middle, and toward the end of your copy. Make sure the copy is written to include the keywords so text flows and sounds natural. You can use free keyword tools, such as the Google AdWords™ Keyword Tool, or you can hire a professional keyword or SEO professional to help you come up with a list of keywords to include on the site.

If your event pertains to a confined geographic area, include keywords that speak about the area that covers your reach. You also should use the keywords in the page titles, headlines, and subheads in the copy on each page.

Marketing messaging

To start building a solid marketing foundation, one of the first tasks is to determine your marketing message. A marketing message is the signal you want to send to anyone who is currently on your lead list as a potential attendee, as well as any potential attendees that have not registered yet. Some marketing professionals refer to this as a positioning statement because it is a written statement that "positions" your event and how you want it to come across to clients.

After you get your positioning statement in order, you will want to establish one to three key messages to send to current and potential attendees through your marketing efforts. These key marketing messages directly promote the benefits that attendees will enjoy, but they are not taglines or memorable and catchy phrases. Instead, you want the audience to walk away with these messages after reading your marketing collateral.

To create your own key messages, list the three primary topics you plan to offer. Under each topic, list how these topics benefit attendees. Now form messages with the topics and the benefits that you want visitors to walk away with after exposure to your marketing initiatives.

Website

Having a business website or Web page devoted to the event is an essential component of promoting events. Getting the event website up and running boils down to two main options: You either can build and maintain the website yourself or hire a professional to build and maintain it for you.

Myriad options exist online for website companies that offer templates you can use to customize the look and feel of your event website. Other sites allow you to host your site with them and build your own site with a desktop publishing or design program. Taking this route might cost you anywhere from $4.95 per month to about $50 per month, depending  on the Web host you choose and the service options you choose to use through the host — such as memory storage amount, email addresses, template options, and the domain name.

The other main option is to hire a Web designer to custom design a site for the event. The cost for a custom website design can run anywhere from $100 for a basic site to thousands of dollars for a complex site. Consider the cost of hiring a designer to create the site and the fact that most designers charge you for making changes to the site after it is up and running.

If it is within your budget, choose a custom site for your initial design, though this will make any changes and maintenance needs difficult. Let the professionals do what they do best: building a strong website. After the design of the site is settled, also consider how you are going to obtain the content for the site. You either have to write the content on your own or hire a writer to create the content for you. This can be an added expense of anywhere from $100 to thousands of dollars, depending on how many Web pages of content are involved.

A basic website for an event has at least four website pages. You should have a home page, which provides a brief overview of the event: the who, what, when, where, and why of the event.

You also should have an About Page. This page should discuss the history of the company, association, organization, or professional that is hosting the event. This page also should include the experience of the event host to add credibility to why the host is the best host to offer the information.

The third page is the topics or sessions page. This page should list out each speaker, session, or workshop of the event. Include the title of each talk and a brief, one paragraph description of what an attendee can expect to take away from the session. Provide information and even headshots for the people that will be leading these sessions so that it illustrates how their expertise benefits attendees.

The final page should be a Contact Us page or Registration page, which should include all your contact information, such as phone number, email address, and address, if you have a physical location. Also, include registration information on this page so that you have a way for visitors to register online or download the registration form and mail it in.

Brochures

Some event promoters find it helpful to have an event brochure, which can be used in various marketing initiatives, from handing them out at trade shows to including them in marketing kits, media professionals, or potential attendees. You even might have two brochures: one that speaks directly to prospective attendees and one that speaks to registered attendees.

As is the case with creating a logo, you can design and print brochures for your staffing business in a variety of ways. The most expensive way to obtain brochures is to hire a graphic designer to design the business cards and then send the file off to a printer to have the brochures printed.

Vistaprint® and 48hourprint.com® also provide customizable brochure templates and printing options. These sites allow you to design your own brochure, add the content, and print the quantity you need at a reduced rate compared to most local printers. You also can opt to have a professional design the brochure or use desktop publishing software to create your own brochure layout and then upload the design to one of these websites to print the brochures.

Last, you can buy brochure card stock that is scored for folding at your local office supply or stationery store. Use a desktop publishing program or templates to customize your brochures, and print them using your home computer and printer. Although this method can be highly cost effective and you can print brochures as you need them rather than having to order hundreds or thousands at a time, it is important that the brochures do not lose their professional appearance. If your brochure looks anything less than professional, it might turn prospects away from registering.

Marketing kits

For intangible and high-ticket events, you have to impress potential attendees more than a tangible product-based business to get them to register. Putting together a marketing or information kit provides you with the opportunity to impress, motivate, and sell by providing your audience with more information than is possible to fit in a standard brochure.

Marketing kits can be a powerful tool to convert sales; leave the kit as a takeaway from a prospect meeting, or drop it in the mail as a follow-up to a phone conversation or in response to an email request from a prospect for more information. A few key essentials are needed for your marketing kit:

Folder — To build a marketing kit, you need a folder or some sort of holder for the marketing information. Keep in mind that the container the marketing kit comes in is the first impression your prospects receives, so you want it to look professional. You can accomplish this in one of two ways. First, you have the option of having folders professionally printed for less with online printers. A less expensive option is to have a label professionally printed that you can then affix to a linen pocket folder.

USP — Create a unique selling proposition (USP). The USP is a brief, one-to five-sentence statement that directly tells readers why your event is different from your competitors' events. In other words, make your event stand out from competitive events. Make sure that your USP is included as part of the marketing kit information. Make sure you word it so that it shows how attending your event benefits attendees from their point of view.

Sell the benefits — Most event promoters provide a list of features rather than the benefits an attendee enjoys by participating in the event. When you list a workshop, topic, or session in your marketing kit, describe how the sessions benefit the attendee by revealing how they resolve an issue, challenge, or problem they are facing.

Session offering — Include a bulleted list that allows the prospect to see your session offering at a quick glance. Follow the bulleted list with a more descriptive list of the seminars, sessions, or workshops at the event.

Testimonials — If it is not your first time hosting this event, previous attendee testimonials can sell your event better than anything you can say to prospects. Include a full page of attendee testimonials, or have your attendees record testimonials that you then include on a DVD or CD as part of the marketing kit.

Articles or media coverage — Third-party endorsements from the media can also pack a powerful sales punch and should be included in the marketing kit. Include reprints of articles published about your event; DVDs of media interviews; or newspaper, magazine, or online article clips where you have been quoted as an expert source or your event is mentioned. This is information you would need to gather at the previous event you hosted or as things come out after that event. Primarily, this is for promoters, organizations, and associations that hold annual or regular events for attendees.

Online Marketing

Through your online marketing efforts, you are trying to accomplish two goals. The ultimate goal is to move visitors from the event website to register as attendees. As you are working to attract new visitors to your site and add these visitors to your list, you simultaneously are working to nurture these leads by communicating with them in an effort to convert them from leads on your list to attendees at your event. Here are some ways to keep attendees and potential attendees up to date:

E-newsletter — Regularly publish an email newsletter to create an automatic lead-capturing system online and as a communication tool for your existing database. You can provide how-to articles, tips, and advice for candidates on event information topics. You also can include news that relates to the topics you are covering at your event. You even might list up-to-date changes on sessions, try to promote the sale of tickets for social events taking place at the event or other information that pertains to attendees.

Editorial calendar — Create an editorial calendar to map out discussion topics for the next six weeks or so. Block out time on your calendar each week to create this content for your newsletters. You also can use existing content you have — such as products, presentations, and reports — to break down and turn into articles and sections of the newsletter. Each article or tip you include in the newsletter should be about 200 to 400 words. The editorial calendar also can be used for creating blog posts, if you decide to start and run a blog, and social media updates. You even can ask your speakers, lecturers, and leaders of your event to submit information you can use in the newsletter.

Social media

Harnessing the power of social media outlets drives more targeted traffic to your website, which in turn will drive more attendees to your event. This provides you with the opportunity to communicate with your target market on a more regular basis and in different ways, and it can have a powerful and positive effect on growing your list and event attendance. Social media networks include Facebook, Twitter, LinkedIn, and YouTube®. Each social media network works slightly differently, so you will need to familiarize yourself with each one. The following sections, however, go into detail on how you can use each network as part of your social media marketing efforts.

Facebook fan page

Create a Facebook fan page that speaks directly to your target markets and focuses on the event. On the fan page for your business, also include an opt-in box for your list so visitors immediately can subscribe and be taken to the event website. To build your fan base, include a special announcement in your e-newsletter to drive traffic to the fan page. Be sure to include a link to your fan page in every piece of correspondence you have with your prospects and registered attendees. You are creating a two-way street: driving traffic from social media to your website and vice versa. If you can gather video or audio testimonials from past attendees, these are also ways to let the event speak for itself. If not, then record case studies or scenarios where you can illustrate how the event helped an attendee gain success.

147

You can use the Facebook fan page in various ways, including sharing your blog posts with links to drive prospective and current attendees directly to where the post sits on your site and posing questions to your audience in an effort to engage them and make it more of an interactive experience. This also allows you to evaluate who your audience is on your fan page so you can then work on funneling them into the appropriate registration level for your event. You also can integrate your Twitter account with your fan page so that your updates get more exposure.

Because Facebook limits actual profiles to individuals, it is better practice to create a Facebook fan page or group for your staffing business and integrate your personal Facebook profile with your event's page. Use your personal profile page to talk about your professional relationship to the business, join relevant groups, and RSVP to events that connect to your target market. Join groups or become a fan of any professional organizations you belong to and any of your competitors. Also, integrate your Twitter account with your profile so that your updates get more exposure. Facebook now even allows you to personalize the URL for the Facebook fan page, which is a good way to brand your event.

Twitter

Twitter is another social media marketing tool you can use to promote your event online. Use Twitter to share information related to your event. This helps position you as an expert resource for information without always trying to sell them on the event. Aim for 80 percent information sharing and 20 percent promotion.

You can integrate your tweets with your blog posts and articles, which is a highly effective way to attract followers, and it permits you to communicate with your followers and drive them to your website. Almost all tweets should include a link to a specific blog article, product, or event information on your website. Sharing helpful tips on how to get the most out of the event or how an attendee can resolve a problem on Twitter has to be done within the 140 characters allowed for tweets. Make your tweets intriguing, and then send your followers somewhere they can get more information. Twitter allows you to share information, but your goal is to use it as a tool to drive traffic to the event website — as is the goal with all your social media marketing. Use the "shorten URL" feature on Twitter to keep the length of the URLs as short as possible; bit.ly (**http://bit.ly**) is a URL shortener that also tracks your links and gives you information on how active a link is.

Follow people you admire — such as authors, bloggers, e-zines you read, seminars you attend, or leaders in your field — as well as your competitors. Visit these profiles and their lists of followers to find people to follow that fit your target market. Consider having a custom background created that matches the event branding, in addition to the sidebar information about your event. A dramatic or attractive background can boost interest for followers.

LinkedIn

LinkedIn is another online source for professionals, business owners, and entrepreneurs. Add a direct link to your website's home page in your profile so that people can take advantage of your early-bird offer right away. Your LinkedIn profile should connect to your blog for further exposure. Start connecting with individuals in related businesses. This is a good way to connect with possible joint venture partners, potential clients, and other referral sources. Also, look for people located in the geographic area where the event is located.

LinkedIn provides a built-in application for gathering recommendations from attendees. Spend some time once per quarter gathering recommendations from your contacts. LinkedIn can be a powerful tool, especially after you have connected with at least 500 other professionals. Even if you cannot get recommendations, use LinkedIn as a tool to connect with your target audiences.

YouTube

Create and use a free YouTube account to upload instructional videos that speak on a certain point of interest to your target audiences. You also can turn each of your written blog posts and/or e-newsletter articles into a video. You are providing just enough information to encourage your audience to gain more information by going to your website. These videos also can be added to your Facebook profile and fan page for additional exposure.

You want to be everywhere that your target audience is, and your target market is using these social media websites.

Blog

Having an up-to-date blog is one of the primary ways people are going to find your event online because search engines look for updated content when determining page rank. Share your expertise about your event, business, industry, or niche in your blog posts. Then, integrate your blog with the social media sites (Facebook, LinkedIn, Twitter) to help drive traffic to your site. Mix it up between longer, more word-driven posts talking about industry-specific news and shorter posts about a  new session or topic that has been added to the event agenda. Any videos or images you can add will also add dimension to your blog. Use complimentary blogging platforms, such as WordPress (**www.wordpress.com**) or Blogger (**www.blogger.com**) to create and maintain a blog.

For a blog to be an effective marketing tool, it is imperative for you to post on your blog at least two to three times a week. Blog posts should include keywords that your target markets use to find information on the event you are hosting. You also can map out six months to a year's worth of e-newsletter content, tweets, and public relations campaigns that are all built around the same editorial content topics to keep everything streamlined and in alignment.

Article marketing

Use content you have created or those that your speakers have created, and develop it into new articles. Aim for at least one article per week. Popular topics for events include how-to articles and articles that cover specific steps or detailed information on topics relevant to your audience.

Use these articles to disseminate information via your e-newsletter, upload them to article directories, such as EzineArticles® (**www.ezinearticles.com**) and Amazines (**www.amazines.com**), use them on your blog, and post them on your social media networks. Make sure your articles are also rich with keywords. Article marketing is one of the most effective and least expensive ways to drive targeted traffic to the event website. Your goal in using article marketing is to drive visitors to the appropriate page of your site. Your goal is to get them to request more information or register for the event. Do this by including a strong call to action in the resource box of each article you submit online. This is also a lead-in for other marketing communication efforts to convert them into attendees.

Also, record the articles you write and repurpose them into videos and podcasts. Upload the podcasts to your blog and create an audio or video series that you can include on your blog, distribute in your e-newsletter, upload to YouTube, or send out as a special series of email blasts to your subscriber list. Podcasts also can be uploaded and distributed on iTunes®.

Link building

On a weekly basis, visit the business websites, blogs, and forums related to your event, niche, or industry. These are additional places where your audience is looking for information and another place where you can find information, as well as build relationships with potential attendees. Post a relevant, valuable comment on at least five sites per week. Forums and blog posts allow you to post your name, business name, and a link back to your event site — again, driving traffic back to your website. This is an indirect way of promoting your event by positioning yourself as an expert and a resource while creating additional exposure for the event. You want your name, event name, and Web address all over the sites that have anything to do with your event. If your potential attendees are visiting these sites, you want them to see you there, too.

Sites of this nature also might offer an opportunity for you to become a guest author or article contributor, which allows you to use content you have to share your expertise with a new audience, gain the attention of your target market by positioning yourself as the expert, and broaden your reach.

Direct response

Also, focus on nurturing the existing leads you have and the new ones you are gathering by consistently communicating with your database. Communicate with your database by sending out auto-responders and promotional email at least once or twice a month. Promotional email might include a special offer on registering for the event, announce the dates of an upcoming event, or incorporate a case study that illustrates a problem one of your attendees faced and how the event resolved the problem. Promotions and case studies also can be included in the e-newsletter.

Event listings

Look for directories, online calendars, and online event listings. These directories, calendars, and listings are often free to add your event. The list is also categorized by days or types of events, so that it is easy for visitors to find events they might have an interest in attending. Some of the sites do charge a nominal fee to add your event. Before you decide to pay for this type of listing, do your homework, as you would before deciding to pay for any type of marketing or promotional tactic.

Find out how many visitors come to the site, daily, weekly, and monthly. Obtain the demographics on these visitors, so you know where they live, work, and play. Find out their professions and household makeups, ages, incomes, and other information that helps you determine that your target audience is using this site.

One of the biggest benefits to listing your event on these sites is SEO and gaining rank in the search engines. Directories, listings, and calendars are popular with the search engines because these types of sites have regular changes to the content. When these sites get a boost in the search engine rankings, then your site can receive a boost as well if it is listed on the site.

Cross-marketing with speakers

Find out what type of online marketing your speakers do to promote the events where they are speakers. If they send out an e-newsletter to their database, ask them to include your event information in the e-newsletter, or send out an email marketing campaign to their list about the event. They even might be willing to hand out promotional information to your event at other speaking engagements they have booked with the same target audience. They might have to obtain approval from that show promoter, but it is a good way to ensure that they have full rooms when speaking at your event. It also helps you promote your event at little or no cost to you.

Offline Marketing

Now that you have a variety of ways you can market your event online, it is time to look at the avenues available for marketing the event offline.

List building

Although you can build your list numerous ways using online marketing tactics, you can build your list just as many ways with offline marketing tactics. The best way to build your list is to combine your online and offline list building efforts. Some of the ways you can build your list offline include:

- Be a guest or participate in as many webinars as possible.

- Be a regular guest on various Internet radio shows.

- Advertise with organizations and associations targeting your target markets.

- Interview well-known people in your niche, and post these interviews online and in print publications.

- Submit articles to print publications that your target market reads.

- Advertise in print publications that your target market reads.

- Do a postcard mailing to a high-quality mailing list, such as attendees from the event for the previous year.

- Attend live networking events and seminars that cater to your target market.

- Periodically ask past and current attendees for referrals.

Public relations program

One of the key programs to boost your event registrations and subscriber list while increasing credibility is publicity. Publicity is a low-cost, effective way to reach your target audience. The purpose of publicity for an event is:

- To inform potential attendees and referral sources about the event and how it can help them

- To educate the media and potential attendees to shape attitudes and behaviors and change perceptions about the industry

- To communicate your marketing messages effectively

Public relations is one of the easiest, most cost-effective ways to promote who you are and what you do so that you can get more registrants for the event. It is a marketing effort that builds credibility and visibility. The art of building favorable and profitable interest is creating a "buzz" in the marketplace, which is what public relations is all about. It is a way of getting your message across to tell others about the event and why it is important to them. Public relations lends credibility from a third-party point of view; therefore, it is often more valuable than advertising alone. It is an effective form of marketing because it:

- Creates awareness of your brand

- Communicates the benefits of your event

- Positions the event host as an expert

- Generates leads and registrations

PR is free and lends more credibility to your claims than paid advertisements. It is the most cost-effective way to generate event interest and reach existing and potential attendees. When people read about the event in the media from a journalist or hear about it on the radio, it receives instant third-party validation and expert positioning. Although a paid advertisement placed in a publication can cost you tens of thousands of dollars each time it is run, a well-placed article is much more cost effective and adds value.

Trade publications have a number of subscribers, and most have thousands of readers, each of whom is a prospect that might benefit from attending the event. At the least, the readers likely know someone who could benefit from attending the event. In addition, this positions you as an expert, which produces a premium price for the event because people are more willing to pay more for expertise. This often removes price as an obstacle to overcome in the process of attracting new attendees. PR also levels the playing field and allows small events to appear larger than they are and compete on the same level as larger events.

PR helps you attract qualified prospects and leads. The more people know about you, the higher the level of trust it builds, which makes it more likely that they will contact you and refer others to you. As an added bonus, registered attendees receive the confirmation they need that they are doing the right thing by attending the event. Here is how to get started:

Develop a media list — A media list should include local and national outlets that will have an interest in covering the event. It is important to find individual reporters, journalists, and writers for the publication that would have an interest in covering your story. You will need to gather and maintain a PR contact list for these local journalists and publications, either by paying for these subscriptions or doing independent research online.

Implement editorial calendars — Most print publications publish a calendar outlining topics they will be covering throughout the year, called an editorial calendar. Use the editorial calendars of your top media outlets to help you develop story ideas for promoting your event. These lists are useful when pitching story ideas, so you can tie in your story with these topics. Also, monitor and identify publicity opportunities from journalists and lists, such as Help a Reporter

Out (**http://helpareporter.com**) and Pitch Rate (**http://pitchrate.com**). Your credibility and reputation only can build if you are positively quoted in a news article.

Write a pitch — Your pitch should be personalized to the person to which you are pitching the story. Mention similar stories he or she has covered, or point out why his or her readers would be interested in the story you have to tell. The pitch also should include an overview of the story and the press release attached for more details.

To start, determine the top three local media outlets for newspaper, TV, and radio in the area where you are hosting the event. Send press releases to specific journalists or editors, and follow up accordingly.

Write a monthly press release — Send out one press release per month for special events, workshops, or webinars you are promoting. An easy strategy, if you do not have something specific to promote for the month, is to use your blog or monthly e-newsletter articles as a press release. This way, you leverage your writing and are able to use your content in multiple places and for multiple purposes.

When writing a press release for online media, the main goal is to have search engines pick up your keywords. An SEO press release is geared toward specific keywords rather than a specific story idea. SEO press releases are written and used online to increase the amount of traffic you drive to your website. Keyword-focused press releases are distributed through wire services. Many companies — especially larger ones — are sending press releases through these online services for the primary purpose of driving traffic to their websites. Submit your monthly press releases to the top five online press release distribution sites, which include one paid service and four free services.

ONLINE PRESS RELEASE DISTRIBUTION CHANNELS	
PRWeb.com	$159/release
I-newswire.com	Free
IdeaMarketers.info	Free
Free-press-release.com	Free
24-7pressrelease.com	Free

Pitch to the media and follow up frequently — Once a month, when you write the press release, pitch the story to the appropriate media outlets. Follow up with each media contact you have pitched the story to, and make sure they received the information. Use the follow-up as an opportunity to see if they are interested in covering the story.

Speaking opportunities

Speaking opportunities can be an excellent source for new prospects and attendee conversions. Use speaking opportunities to expand your reach and position yourself as an expert in your field, or tell how the experts in the field will be sharing information at your upcoming event. Off-site speaking engagements help you reach potential attendees. Some options include being a guest speaker for radio shows, webinars, and workshops — online or live. Speaking engagements allow you to connect face-to-face with current and potential attendees and referral sources.

Have a system in place to gather the names and contact information of the attendees of the show or event where you are speaking. Run a contest to gather names, email addresses, and telephone numbers. This allows you to build your list of leads and provides you with the opportunity to follow up with those leads to try to convert them into attendees. Run a show or speaking engagement special so that if someone registers, he or she receives a special discount or bonus offer.

A large amount of planning and effort goes into planning a workshop, seminar, or event of this nature. Marketing and promoting the event is one of the biggest factors in landing people in these seats and ensuring that your event is a smashing success. When you use a combination of online and offline marketing tactics to get in front of your target markets, it increases your chances of converting prospects into registrants for your event.

Controlling marketing costs

Marketing is essential to your event's success and your overall business's well being, but it also can be a budget buster. Your annual marketing plan is likely to include the telephone book's Yellow Pages and similar publications. Avoid the temptation to go for a full-page advertisement, despite what a salesperson may tell you about its benefits. You will want a Yellow Pages presence, but you do not need to spend big dollars. There can be a significant lag-time for such annual ads, especially since your event, seminar, and workshops' calendar is continuously changing. If your business is like most startups, you will have a limited marketing budget. It is advisable to spread it around to get the best value. The only marketing that is worthwhile *makes you money.*

Whether you are the speaker for the event or you have multiple speakers, once you fill the seats at the event, everyone in the audience is waiting for you to deliver what they came there to learn. *In Chapter 8, you will uncover some of the different formats for delivering the information to the audience and evaluate whether the delivery was a success or might need some additional work for next time.*

Chapter Eight
Deliver

Once you and your speakers are standing in the spotlight, make sure you deliver what your audience is there to receive. Chapter 8 covers all the essentials of implementing the workshops and seminars on the day or days of the event. This includes advice on delivering the information, how  to deal with questions from attendees, the notes to take while the seminar is unfolding, how to maintain the audience, and even recording what you do for further evaluation or to sell as an information product at a later time. Additionally, you will learn some tips for leading simulations or exercises, tips for "teaching" for the first time, advice on speaking, and how to manage your time.

Formats for Delivering the Information

Even the most outgoing and social individuals might freeze the first time they stand up in front of a group of attendees. It is a normal reaction to be nervous. The more group speaking you do, the less likely you are to experience stage fright. Whether it is your first time or your 100th time speaking, here are some tips and tidbits of advice to help ensure your session is a raging success:

One of the easiest ways for participants to learn at seminars and workshops is through a simulation process. A simulation allows the attendees to break up into small groups to learn how something works with some hands-on work of their own. The simulation process requires the group  members to "build" a machine, for example. After building the machine, they now have a much better handle on what the machine is made of, which also helps them better understand what the machine can do.

After building the machine, the group participants then can work on other factors that directly relate to the machine, such as ways to improve the quality of the output of the machine or ways to solve other problems machine users might be experiencing. The bottom line is that by actively engaging the participants, they are learning the concept you are trying to teach by "building" it from the ground up.

Another aspect of this type of learning is using questions to help stimulate the group discussion. Thought-provoking questions quickly engage the audience and can get the creative juices flowing in their mind. Throw a question out to the audience, and then pause for a few seconds. You will see recognition wash over several faces in the group. Suddenly, hands will shoot up to provide you with the answer to your question.

To foster a true learning environment, it is less about the "teacher" and more about the "student." You are an expert in your field, but your attendees will learn more from your experience when you give them the tools they need and then put them in the driver's seat to drive their learning experience to understanding.

CASE STUDY: INNOVATIVE FORMATS THAT GUARANTEE INTERACTION AND LEARNING

Valentine Global, LLC
Chike Uzoka
P.O. Box 32341
Newark, NJ 07102
(732) 778-2538
www.chikeuzoka.com

Valentine Global, LLC, is a consulting firm that creates and facilitates age-appropriate and interactive entrepreneurship workshops, seminars, classes, and games for people of all ages. Valentine Global has a book series geared to teaching young men everything from entrepreneurship and life skills to the how to manage the high school and college experience. Valentine Global works with clients in New Jersey, New York, Washington D.C., California, and Atlanta, Georgia.

Generally, the profiles for the attendees at the workshops are simple — anyone age 3 to 103. For the most part, the workshop participants and attendees are already affiliated with the Valentine Global clients' organizations. Valentine Global works with small- and medium-sized companies, school systems, mentoring organizations, and nonprofits in urban and suburban communities.

The delivery of the information is what Valentine Global says sets their events apart from the rest. The company philosophy is telling someone something and showing them are two different things. Rather than focusing on telling attendees how great entrepreneurship is, these events focus on showing attendees what they need to do to launch their own businesses. Valentine Global combines delivery methods in its workshops — sharing information (the tell) and then showing them how to do. Some topics include how to register an LLC online, how to write a business plan, and how to setup social media outlets. Then, Valentine Global provides attendees with the tools attendees should use to be successful.

> The "Handling Your Business" workshop campaign has proven successful online and offline. Its purpose is to bring in more clients and more strategic partnerships. Using the company website, Facebook, Twitter, and LinkedIn pages in conjunction for its "Handling Your Business" campaign helped capture more clients in an effort to reach more people. The company uses its Facebook page to create picture albums showcasing the seminars and workshops. They have found that Twitter is a great tool that allows the company to disseminate message to different people in different countries in a relatively short amount of time. The LinkedIn profile focuses on attracting more corporate clients to create entrepreneurship workshops and workshops on topics, such as sales, time management, and soft skills.

Tips for "teaching"

Learning is more about the student than it is the teacher. You can stand in front of attendees and teach them everything you know. Most will forget what you have said in two seconds or less. Others diligently will write down what you say, only to take it back  home or to the office to do nothing with it. When you truly engage your audience and make it more of an interactive experience, attendees tend to learn better and retain more of the information. This is what ultimately makes you the best "teacher" in your field.

Here are the top ten tips on "teaching," gathered from numerous professional speakers, experience, and common sense.

1. **Turn it into a game** — Formats such as Jeopardy®, Wheel of Fortune® and Card Sharks® are game shows you can use to share the information

you want to provide, while fostering a fun learning environment at the same time. This format takes some planning on your part because you have to set up the "game board" for each type of show. This also adds a competitive feeling to the room, and people love to compete with each other and win. This solves the problem of keeping your audience engaged, and it alleviates you from having to stand at the front of the room and continuously ramble on about your topic.

2. **Tune up** — Add music to the mix. Choose music selections based on the activity or portion of the session. For example, when attendees are entering the room and finding their seats, play mellower selections. During breakout sessions, where you have broken the large group of attendees down into smaller groups, play fast-paced music in the background to spur creativity and thinking. It is a similar philosophy to shopping. Stores that want to stimulate impulse buys from shoppers tend to play fast-paced and loud music.

3. **Create a mix of techniques** — Another way to keep up the pace and maintain the audience's attention is mix up your techniques, so that you are using two or more different teaching styles. For example, you might spend the first 60 minutes of a two-hour session lecturing. This provides the audience with the information they need to then move on to the remainder of the session, which is a game show where they will use what you taught them to try to win. During your lecture, pass out handouts, use a PowerPoint presentation, or throw out questions to help guide the discussion.

4. **Personalize for the group** — When you are speaking for a specific company or association, try to get to know something about the employees, group members, or the executives of the organization. Use the key information you find out about these individuals to incorporate it into your speaking engagement. Find out about a recent initiative the

company implemented or a cause that the group is passionate about. Again, leverage this information to create a personalized presentation, using some of this custom information in your presentation. The audience relates much better to something they can identify with than using examples.

5. **Tell a story** — The point of any good story is to relate information to the listener. Rather than throw out a bunch of concepts at the audience, incorporate the concepts you are trying to teach and tell a real story about one of your clients that used the ideas. You also can get creative and find a fairy tale that you can use as the basis for the story. Change the storyline enough to fit the information you are trying to teach, but your audience members are sure to be on the edge of their seats as you tell the story. This scenario is leading by example because it puts an interesting spin on the facts and figures you are trying to get across to the audience.

6. **Have breakout sessions** — When you are lecturing or speaking, you tend to get egocentric and caught up in yourself. When you break up the attendees into small groups, it gives them an opportunity to apply what they have learned. Additionally, the group members also tend to learn from their peers. These types of activities should reinforce the information you share with the group as a whole.

7. **Role-play** — Role-play is a specific type of small group activity, but it provides benefits. Role-play allows you and the other participants to personalize the concept you are teaching to a specific situation. For example, you might lecture about handling a specific situation when the business owner is selling a product. The majority of attendees, however, might be selling a service. During role-play, the concept can be modified to fit a service-based business rather than a product-based business. Additionally, role-play activities allow participants to apply what they have learned to a specific situation. The application portion of

the learning process, rather than just listening to someone talk, tends to engage additional learning.

8. **Be visual** — You are likely to have different types of users in the audience. Some can learn by listening to what you say, but many attendees are visual learners. Even those that are auditory learners can benefit from your use of visual aids. Use pictures, handouts, projections, PowerPoint slides, videos, or any other visual aids that might to the concept you are teaching. Again, these visuals reinforce the concepts and topics you are covering in your lecture.

9. **Handouts** — When you use handouts, you accomplish two things. First, you have a visual aid that helps attendees learn. More important, when you hand a handout to each attendee yourself, you have the opportunity to get in front of each attendee and talk.

10. **Use the team approach** — Rather than having one person stand at the front of the room and speak for one to two hours straight, use a team approach. Work with the team ahead of time to plan how this will work, but break up the two-hour session for the speakers and the attendees. Just as one speaker might be losing the attention of some of the audience, a new speaker comes on, which causes movement and change in the room and re-engages the audience.

Advice on speaking

Everyone is not born to be a public speaker. The good news is that you can learn the skills it takes. The previous section gave you some ideas on how to engage your audience and how to maximize a learning environment. Now, focus on some of the speaking techniques and tactics you can use to sharpen or improve the delivery of your lecture, discussion, or speech.

Practice, practice, and then practice again

The biggest piece of advice you can take from professional speakers is that you must practice. The old adage, "Practice makes perfect" does apply here. You never want the first time you are giving a lecture or speech to be when you stand up in front of the audience. It might sound quirky, but set up your living room, office, or bedroom similar to how the room will be on the day of your event. There is no need to go overboard, but have the basics, such as your presentation, notes, and handouts, available.

If you have a video camera and/or audio recorder, set these up as well. Go through your presentation, just as you would if you were delivering it right now to the intended audience. The benefits of recording your delivery are that you can sit down, watch it, and listen to it yourself. Do not cringe at this idea because it is your opportunity to pick up things that you still have time to alter and correct before you do them in front of a room full of people.

Jot down notes on any modifications that you think you should make to your delivery. Here is a hint: If you are falling asleep or bored by your own presentation, then it is highly likely that your attendees are going to feel the same way. Now is the time to figure out ways you can make your delivery more appealing, more desirable, more exciting, and in a way that fosters learning and retention of the information.

If you are incorporating role-playing, simulations, and small-group activities into your speech, then you are not going to be able to practice this. You can, however, practice the directions and breaking to give the groups time to form and start on the activity.

Practice in front of people

Assemble a group of people for your practice. If this is a work speech, then assemble employees or colleagues. You can also assemble a group of people that you know, such as your family members and friends. It is imperative that you assemble a group of people who will offer you suggestions and feedback and who will be honest with  you. In other words, if you are the boss, assembling people who work for you might not be the best idea. They might be afraid to provide you with honest feedback if the feedback is negative. It defeats the purpose of practicing in front of a group, and getting them to give you input if the input is not real and honest.

Elicit and incorporate feedback

Make sure that you talk with the group you have assembled before and after your presentation. Encourage them to take notes. Ask them to jot down any positive feedback, but also ask them to write down constructive criticism on things that you could do better. Let them know not to interrupt you while you are giving your talk but to hold everything they have collected until the end. Run through the practice in front of the group just like you will on the day of the event.

At the end, have a group discussion on their thoughts. Especially when more than one person in the room agrees on a point, figure out ways you can incorporate the change. The pretend attendees might have suggestions, or you might have to come up with ways to make the changes on your own.

After you walk away from the group practice session or watch yourself and provide your own feedback, then it is time to incorporate the feedback into changes in your presentation.

Practice more

Once you have all the changes made to the presentation, then practice again. Even if you do not have any changes (which is unlikely), or you only have one or two changes, it is imperative that you continue to practice until you could do the presentation in your sleep. The more you practice, the more likely you are to get through your presentation with few mistakes on the day of the event, and the more natural your presentation will come across.

How to manage your time

Time management is one of the biggest factors when giving a presentation. You have a time slot and allotment of time to cover what you need to cover and have attendees participate in any discussions or activities. The first and best way to manage your time is to practice. When practicing your speech or lecture, use a stopwatch or timer to help you pace yourself.

At the halfway point of your presentation, do a quick check of the watch, stopwatch, or timer to make sure you at least have half your time left. You also might want to save some time at the end to answer any lingering questions attendees might have. You will notice that when you first start practicing, it might take you longer to get through the presentation and that you start and stop more often. As you continue to practice and truly learn the material, you will notice this cuts down on the amount of time it takes you to deliver the information, as well as the number of times you have to stop and start again.

If you are still running over your time after you continue to practice, then you might have to consider cutting out or cutting back on certain areas of your presentation. First, see if there are ways you can get the same point across in a more direct manner. If  not, then take out any portions that are not absolutely necessary or beneficial to the audience.

It is acceptable on the day of the event to set up indicators so that you know how you are doing on time. First, you can use your watch or a stopwatch that you keep at the podium or near where you are presenting. Avoid constantly checking your time because this can be distracting to the audience. At about the halfway point of your presentation, do a quick check to see how you are doing on time. This check alerts you to whether you can continue at the same pace or if you need to slow down or speed up a bit.

You also might want to plant a timekeeper in the audience. They do not necessarily have to sit through your entire speech, but have them come in and raise their hand in the back when you should be halfway through the presentation. This way, you know, but nobody else does, that you have half your time left. This person is a member of your staff or the event staff, rather than an actual audience member. You also might opt for both options. Keep track of your own time, and employ a timekeeper in the audience.

Last, hold off answering audience questions until the end. If you allow attendees to interrupt what you are saying to answer their question, this can throw you off track — mentally and time wise. When you open the session, ask everyone to hold their questions until the end, and leave the last five or ten minutes of the session to answer as many questions as you can. Any other people with questions that you do not get to answer in the public forum always have the option of speaking to you at the end.

Q&A Sessions

Some events are solely question-and-answer sessions. For these types of events, you do not have a formal speech or lecture but instead allow the questions attendees have to control the flow of the conversation. If this is the type of session you are having, go in prepared with a few questions as jumping off points, just in case someone does not immediately raise his or her hand with a burning question for you to answer and get the discussion going.

Attendees might need clarification on a point you made during your discussion or want to ask something that you did not cover in your lecture. When you are timing your presentation, make sure to end it with enough time to allow for questions at the end. Since you are taking questions at the end, instruct the audience not to interrupt with questions while you speak. This permits you to stay on your schedule without having to start and stop. Suggest that they jot the question down when it occurs to them so that they do not forget it by the time the question-and-answer portion rolls around.

Take Notes during the Seminar

As you are setting up for the event, as the event is happening, and during the teardown of the event, keep notes on what is going right, what is going wrong, and what things might need some tweaking. Have the other event staff members jot down notes as well. You can gather all this information in a "post-mortem" meeting. Everyone involved in the event can participate in a conference call or meet face-to-face to discuss their personal observations, suggestions, and feedback.

You can use this information when planning your next seminar, workshop, conference, or event.

Record the Event

Another good way to look back on the event is to record everything you can — especially the information sessions. Set up or have the audiovisual professionals set up and record each session of the event. You and your staff members can watch these videos later to critique the event as a whole. You might recognize things that were good and identify things that could have been done better. When you collect the feedback forms from attendees, you will see some of the same feedback that you observed but you will likely see other feedback as well.

Additionally, when you videotape the information sessions, speeches, lectures, and exercises, you also can create an information product to sell. Members of your target market that could not attend the event, for example, can buy the edited and taped version of the sessions and obtain the information, just as if they were in the same room. Although it will cost you money to tape, edit, and package the DVDs, videos, or audio files, these information products are also a way to boost the revenue of the event.

Now, you should be prepared to deliver your own presentation. You have advice, tips, and tricks used by professional speakers, seminar, and workshop hosts. It is important to keep in mind that no event ever comes off without a hitch.

In Chapter 9, you will learn how to create a positive and working relationship with the seminar, workshop, or conference attendees.

Chapter Nine

Working with Attendees

Once the attendees register for the event, it is your responsibility to help guide them in getting to the event. Whether it is local or long-distance travel, this chapter covers how to create attendee information packets to provide travel information, hotel suggestions, and local city information. If it is an event where the hosts are arranging travel for the attendees, then the information packets will include this type of information. Information packets also should include transportation information from the nearby airports to the hotel where the seminars and workshops are scheduled or transportation options from other hotels to the event venue. The packet should include the agenda for the event so that attendees will know what to expect and can coordinate their schedules accordingly.

Registration Packets

Once an attendee signs up to attend the event, the registration packet goes out with all the information he or she will need. The two biggest portions of the registration packet are travel information and the agenda for the workshop, seminar, or conference. One of the items you should include in the registration packet is a confirmation letter. Similar to the letter you send to speakers, this letter thanks the attendee for registering and sets some basic ground rules so that the event is a successful one for them and the rest of the participants.

A sample letter might look something like this:

July 12, 2013

Seminars 'R Us
1234 XYZ St.
Anytown, MI USA 55555

Dear Kenneth:

Thank you for attending this event!

Your money and time are important to you. For this reason, we are dedicated to packing this seminar full of relevant and useful information that you can use right away. We have an excellent lineup of speakers and professional running our sessions and workshops. They are ready and willing to share their knowledge with you, so that you can hit the ground running as soon as you leave the event.

We also need to ask for your help in making this event as successful as possible — not only for you but for everyone involved in the event.

Problems, Questions & Information

Problems, questions and the need for information is a common issue participants at events have. For this reason, we have set up an information table conveniently located near the registration desk near the Amelia Ballroom of the hotel. The information table is staffed during all hours of the event, so feel free to stop and speak with one of the staff members at the table.

Guidelines to Follow

We also ask each participant to follow these basic guidelines to make the event an enjoyable experience for everyone.

- Please turn your cell phone off before entering each session. Please do not leave it on vibrate because this affects the audiovisual equipment and is still a disruption. If you can put your phone on silence so that it does not make any noise, this is fine. We have built in several breaks throughout the day so that you can check email, messages, and make phone calls.

- Each session will have a Q&A period at the end of the session. If you have a question, please wait for the microphone to be handed to you before asking your question.

- Speakers will be available after sessions and during breaks. If you have a question or are not able to ask a speaker a question during the Q&A session, you will have time to ask speakers during off times.

- Please be in your seat and ready at least five minutes before the scheduled start time. We have two very full days of programming, and we do not want you to miss one minute of this useful and relevant information.

- Network with your peers! You have an opportunity to learn as much from your fellow participants as you do the speakers at the event. Use these opportunities to meet other attendees and discover ways you can help each other, do business with each other, or refer business to each other.

Thank you again for attending this very exciting event. We have worked hard to pack the schedule with a lot of great information. We look forward to seeing you soon!

Sincerely

Jane D. Doe

Jane D. Doe

So that you understand how the process works, let us walk through a quick scenario. After this, you will see the details in helping you put your attendee information packets together for distribution.

Assume you have everything set up for the event registration. Attendees can register online, by phone, or via email. Someone is the point person for all the registrations. It is best to have one person own the entire registration process so that there is a consistent process in place. The registration form comes in and is processed. Processing entails entering the attendee information into the attendee database, processing the payment for the attendee, and sending out the attendee.

Travel Information

For some events, you as the event planner and host are responsible for booking transportation for attendees. In other situations, attendees are responsible for booking their own travel arrangements. Either way, it is a good idea to provide as much useful travel information as possible in the information packets.

Planes, trains, and automobiles

If you are booking travel for the attendees, then include a copy of their travel itinerary for the transportation they need to take to get to the event. This includes any airplane or train itineraries, or rental car confirmations.

If attendees are responsible for their own travel, you still can provide generic information to fit their travel needs. Print a one-page information sheet that includes the name or names of the nearest airports they should consider flying into from out of town. You also can provide the closest train and bus station information to where the event is so that attendees know where to book their inbound and outbound transportation.

Provide a quick list of the rental car locations that service the airports, bus stations, or train stations. You also might want to include rental car agencies that are near the hotel where guests are staying or the location of the event — especially if it is a hotel.

If you have a travel agent the attendees can contact, list the name of the agency, the agent, and the contact information. Tell the attendee to mention the event so that the agent knows what group to book the attendee through and provide any group discounts that you have been able to negotiate. If you are not working with a travel agent but have negotiated discount travel rates, list the discount and discount code the attendee needs to use when booking travel so that the attendee receives the group discount.

Shuttles

Many hotels offer complimentary shuttle service from its location to the airport and from the airport to the hotel. If this is the case, provide shuttle information in the attendee packet. This information might include where to meet the shuttle from the airport and the times the shuttle runs. If it is not a complimentary shuttle but a shuttle service, list the price for taking the shuttle and whether exact change is required, along with the other information about the shuttle.

Taxis

For attendees who require taxi service, add local taxicab information to the sheet. This might include two to four local cab companies that service the area and their contact information.
You might want to give an idea on the rates and the distance from the airport to the hotel.

Local city info

It is also a nice touch to add information about the local area and city where the event takes place. You might want to include a brief history of the town or city, along with some of the top attractions and activities attendees might want to enjoy while they are in town. Add to the list some of the restaurants, coffee shops, and other eateries that are near the hotel where attendees are staying or near the hotel where the event is being held. Often, you can obtain information sheets like this directly from the hotel or from the local tourism bureau.

Workshop/Seminar Agenda

One of the final and most important pieces of information in the packets is the agenda for the workshop, seminar, or conference. You should have a timeline for the arrival date and each day of the event in the packet. Every attendee has the same agenda, so it is just a matter of typing up the agenda and having copies of it made and collated, if necessary.

In situations where agendas vary by participant, then you have to personalize the agenda by attendee. For example, if attendees are assigned to specific breakout sessions, then you will need to indicate this on the attendee's agenda so they know where to go during the time slot of their breakout session.

The more information you can offer your attendees on registration, the less likely you are to be flooded with phone calls asking questions they can find the answers to in their information packets. These packets also set the tone that the event is organized, well thought out, and well planned. This type of information is well received and highly appreciated by your attendees, which sets the tone and mood on arrival for the event.

No matter how much you plan, there are going to be some bumps in the road. The idea is to minimize the problems as much as you can by anticipating what might happen before it happens and how to deal with it when it does happen.

In Chapter 10, you will learn how to create a smooth platform to work on to help you avoid problems and learn how to correct the issues that might arise.

Chapter Ten

Mistakes and Disasters and How to Avoid Them

This chapter covers potential mistakes and disasters that can make or break the event. Learn each possible mistake or disaster and have a plan to avoid them or deal with them if they come up.

Potential Mistakes

Three of the biggest mistakes you can make at the event is get off schedule, lose your audience, or get off the topic. These top three mistakes quickly can cause the entire event to spiral out of control. If you plan for these challenges ahead of time, it helps reduce the chances of these things occurring.

Getting off schedule

Running an event is similar to running a doctor's office. The doctor has a slotted schedule for patients similar to your schedule that includes time slots for every discussion, activity, and break. It only takes one patient spending more time with the doctor than the receptionist allotted for that patient and the patients for the rest of the day find themselves sitting in the lobby and patient rooms longer. It only takes one unexpected building fire alarm or technical problem to throw the rest of your event off schedule.

Although some things might happen that are completely out of your control, focus on the things you can control to help keep your event running on schedule.

- Do a giveaway or special bonus activity at the beginning of the training. This encourages people to show up and be in their seats ready to go at the start time of the session. Use your marketing materials and reminders that go out leading up to the event to announce this.

- Send reminders. Use all the communications you have with your attendees to provide them with a friendly reminder of the start time.

- Offer breakfast 15 to 30 minutes before the session is scheduled to start. This means the majority of the attendees will be in the breakfast room or area where the session is scheduled. You then can direct them into the room five or so minutes before the start time so that everyone is in their seats when the speaker is ready.

- Build some cushion into the agenda. When you are creating the agenda, make sure that you are allocating enough time for sessions and breaks, but not too much time. Also, when allotting time for sessions, do not give the speaker all the time allotted for the session, but rather shave off ten or so minutes from their presentation time. For example, if the session is an hour long, tell the speaker he or she has 50 minutes. This gives you about five extra minutes at the beginning and end of the session to allow for runover in other sessions or other types of delays.

Losing the audience

As the speaker, you will notice if you are losing the attention of your audience. When half or more of them are not paying attention to you, are nodding off in their seats, playing with their cell phones, or talking to the person next to them, they are no  longer listening to you. Instead of losing them further, you might take a moment to recapture their attention. You can do this by moving up the activity you have scheduled, throwing out a question, moving around the room while you talk, or something that changes the dynamic of the room.

If time permits, you also might take this opportunity to give the attendees a break. Make it short, though. Give them five to ten minutes to use the restroom, grab a refreshment, or stretch their legs. If you give them any more than ten minutes, it could be hard to get them back in their seats to restart the session on time.

Talkers can disrupt the entire flow of the session, if you allow them to do so. Audience members holding their own conversations are distracting to you and the other attendees. Try to walk toward the talkers — not in a threatening way. As you walk toward them and continue speaking, this should curtail their conversation. If that does not work, then politely ask if there is a question. They will either say no and stop talking, or they will say yes and you can address the question and regain control of the room. If you have asked them to hold their questions until the end, then remind them of this when they say yes.

Getting off topic

You can control keeping yourself on topic. Stick to the "script" you practiced when preparing for your presentation. Use notes, presentation slides, or handouts to help keep you on track. If you lose your place or forget where you left off, take a moment to look down at your guide and pick up from where you left off. What is harder to control is when an attendee gets you or the rest of the group off the discussion topic.

In this situation, it is up to you to get everyone back on track. For example, if someone asks you a question that will take you off topic, then let the person know that you would be happy to answer the question after the presentation but that it does not pertain to the discussion at hand. If someone in the audience starts talking off topic when sharing with the group, politely bring them to a stopping point and use a transition to get back on topic. You politely can point out that that is out of the realm of discussion, thank them for sharing, and then throw out a question or make a statement so you can pick back up where you left off.

Potential Disasters

Although the potential challenges so far are not earth-shattering, other situations can quickly lead to disaster. Speakers who do not show up for their sessions, technical problems, and disruptive attendees are a few of the top disaster creators at a seminar, workshop, conference, or event. The best way to handle the first two potential disasters is to always have a backup plan. During the preplanning and planning process for the event, put the backup plans in place.

Speakers that don't show up

It is rare that this happens, but it does happen. You have a speaker booked. You have confirmed the speaker is coming to the event, and then he or she simply does not show up. You might even have a speaker that checks into his or her hotel room the night before but is missing in action on the day of the event. The best way to handle this is to have some backup speakers who can speak on the same or a similarly related topic. It might be you or one of the other speakers you have booked for the event but who had a different time slot than the missing speaker.

If you are a speaker, you might have a presentation that you often give. You can slide this presentation into the time slot. Make sure you have any presentation materials you might need with you, just in case. If you cannot speak and/or do not have any backup speakers you can put into the slot, consider switching the session format from a lecture or speech to a discussion or question-and-answer period. You need a moderator to start the discussion or questions and answers going, but you do not necessarily need the expert to talk on the originally scheduled program.

If this happens, be prepared for complaints from attendees. Some attendees might have registered just for this particular session, so when they do not get what they were promised, they might ask for their money back. You might choose to refund all or a portion of their money. You also might offer them a seat at your next event instead. It is up to you how you handle these types of complaints, but those are a few ways to deal with the problem.

Technical problems

One of the most prominent disasters is a technical problem. It could be problems with the projector. It might be that the microphone does not work. It could be that the computer will not boot. No matter how much you test equipment, something may go awry — be it major or minor.

This is where having various types of visual aids comes in handy. If your sole presentation material is a PowerPoint and the computer fails, then you have to talk off the top of your head. If you have a video, handouts, and flip charts, however, then you still can proceed with your presentation with some minor tweaking in the delivery.

If the speaker has a loud enough speaking voice, you might be able to go on without a microphone until the audio specialists can bring in a backup microphone. Make sure that each speaker has a disc or backup of his or her presentation so that another computer can be used in place of the speaker's computer when it is a computer issue.

In other words, think of the potential technical difficulties you might experience and ways to handle them before they happen.

Disruptive attendees

Another problem is a disruptive attendee. He or she might get belligerent to a staff member at the information table or heckle the speaker during a session. How you handle it is situational, but here are some ideas to get your creative juices flowing.

Someone who is disruptive because they are not on the list to get in or have an agenda problem might cause trouble for staff members working the table. Staff members should use common sense and sympathy to handle the problem attendee. Listen to the problem carefully, repeat the problem as they understand it back to the attendee, and then let the attendee know that you will see what you can do to correct it. If it is something that you can fix immediately, simply apologize for the inconvenience, and give them what they want. This is the fastest and easiest way to put an end to the disruption.

Train staff members to call a manager or someone who is charge of the event for any issues they cannot handle on their own. As the event manager, you can determine what is in your power to change for the attendee. If you are not sure of how to correct the problem, ask the attendee what they would like you to do. If what they are asking for is reasonable and in your control, then grant it to them. If it is not, then come up with a logical alternative.

The biggest challenge is handling disruptive attendees inside of the speaking engagements or sessions. Earlier, you learned how to deal with minor disruptions, such as people having side conversations. The type of disruptions here are major ones, such as attendees standing up and yelling or interrupting the speaker, heckling the speaker, and making it impossible for the other attendees to hear and pay attention to the person in charge.

As the speaker, you can make a joke and try to calm the person down. Repeat back to them what their concern is and tell them that you understand what they are saying or that you empathize with their problem. Address it, and then move on. In many circumstances, this works to put the person at ease, quiets them down, and returns them to their seats. If it gets out of hand, you might have to bring in a security person from the venue or hotel to escort a disruptive person out.

The event manager should address the situation with an attendee that has been removed from the session. You can give the attendee an opportunity to get their behavior under control and return to the session, or you can have them escorted off the property altogether.

With a plan in place on how to deal with various issues that might pop up during the event, you are prepared for almost anything. *In Chapter 11, you will learn the steps to take to evaluate your seminar, workshop, or conference.*

☑ AWESOME!

☐ **Excellent**

☐ **Very Good**

☐ **Satisfactory**

☐ **Marginal**

☐ **Poor**

Chapter Eleven
Evaluating the Seminar and Workshop Success

Even after the seminar is over, your work is not done. Have an evaluation process established before you launch the seminar. You want to elicit feedback from the attendees. You also should gather feedback from the event staff. This chapter covers how to put together, distribute, and collect these surveys and questionnaires. Additionally, you will learn how to set measurable goals, profit margins, attendee satisfaction rates, speaker satisfaction rates, and staff satisfaction rates so that you can measure the success rate of the workshop or seminar.

Creating, Distributing, and Collecting Evaluations

Because you have three primary groups of people to survey about the seminar or workshop, you also have three different evaluation forms to create. In addition to creating the actual forms, you also need to consider the best ways to distribute and collect the evaluation forms. To evaluate each part of the evaluation process and prepare to implement the process, it is best to break it down by the three groups: attendees, speakers, and staff.

From the attendees

The attendees are the first primary group of people you want to complete a survey. You should assemble a questionnaire that has attendees rate their experience from their standpoint. When you are assembling the questionnaire, mix multiple-choice questions, questions that use a rating scale, and open-ended questions in the format. You can find a sample attendee questionnaire in Appendix B. Your goal in having attendees complete the survey is to find out which aspects of the seminar or workshop  had a positive experience, and if there were any negative experiences. Attendees also tend to be a good source of suggestions in how you can make the event even better the next time around.

When compiling the survey questions, plot the questions from the first point of contact you have with the attendees to the last touch point. In other words, start questions from their check-in experience, throughout the entire event, and up until the time they walk out the door. For conferences or events where you are responsible for booking travel and accommodations for attendees, include questions that pertain to that part of the process as well.

When it comes to getting the surveys into attendees' hands and getting them to submit them back to you, you have different ways to accomplish this. If there was one big session, then you can have the surveys in the packets that you hand out to attendees when they check in for the event. At the end of the session, have the speaker or someone remind attendees that the sheets are in their packets. Ask them to complete the forms and hand them to the representatives standing at the exit doors on their way out of the room. This provides you with the information right away and tends to have a higher completion rate than if you send the surveys to attendees later.

If the conference or event has multiple sessions, then ideally, provide a survey that allows the attendee to rate each session. You can do this by having one big survey at the end of the conference, or you can have them complete a survey at the end of each session, which just has them rate that particular session. Conducting individual session surveys provides you with a more granular view on the content, setup, and the speaker for the session. You still can have a survey at the end that goes into detail on the event, seminar, workshop, or conference as a whole.

Sending out surveys to attendees after the event is another way to handle surveying attendees. Although this way lacks instant gratification for you, it does allow you to touch base with attendees after the event. Delaying the survey process also provides attendees some time to allow the information to soak in and even implement what they learned from the workshop or seminar, so they can relay this information in their survey responses. You can email the surveys to attendees using an online survey program, or you can send out hard copy forms. If you choose to send a hard-copy format, you can increase the response rate by including a self-addressed stamped envelope for the attendee to return the survey to you.

CASE STUDY: COALITIONS BRING MEMBERS TOGETHER FOR COLLABORATION AND INTERACTION

Independent Mystery
Shoppers' Coalition
Pamela Richardson
25955 Orbita
Mission Viejo, CA 92691
(949) 433-2676
www.imscnews.com

The Independent Mystery Shoppers' Coalition brings mystery shoppers, schedulers, editors, mystery shopping company owners, and their clients together for educational conferences. The seminars and workshops are the primary business plan the coalition uses to bring these industry experts together to allow them to learn and connect.

The workshops and seminars are also a recruiting tool. Describe the process you go through to research and build the profile for the types of attendees that should come to the seminar/workshop. Since mystery shopping is open to people from ages 13 and up, the profiles are as varied as the mystery shops themselves. The coalition staff seeks individuals that are interested in adding to their income by working from home, those who are stay at home parents, retirees, and students. The coalition staff finds these individuals by joining forums that cater to these groups, interacting on social media networks such as Facebook, LinkedIn, and Twitter.

The Independent Mystery Shoppers' Coalition says feedback, feedback, and feedback are the measurable goals set for the seminars and workshops so that you can determine if the event was a success or not. The staff interviews the attendees on site during the event. They ask for their feedback via email, and they monitor what attendees post on the social media networks and forums they visit. Since the majority of the attendees are mystery shoppers or mystery shopping company owners, getting feedback and measuring the success happens rather quickly.

The Independent Mystery Shoppers' Coalition uses seminars and workshops as part of the business and marketing plan because mystery shoppers do not have the ability to see one another on a regular basis. The seminars and workshops create the face-to-face interactions of those in the industry that tend to work alone on a daily basis. When mystery shoppers sit down together for the first time, they realize: "Hey, this person gets it; they understand me." Shoppers meet company owners, schedulers, and editors without the titles attached and connect with them as people. The human factor is alive and well; the changes it brings to everyone who attends creates a bond, one that goes home with them.

From the speakers

The second primary group you want to survey is the speakers at the event. While attendees give you their experience from the audience perspective, the speakers have experiences from a different perspective. The questionnaire for the speakers also should have a mix of questions that include multiple choice questions, rating scales, and open-ended questions. You can find a sample speaker questionnaire in Appendix C. The goal in having speakers complete the survey is to find out which aspects of the seminar, conference, or workshop were positive, which were mediocre, and which areas you might need to put some work into the next time around. Speakers, especially those that speak on a full-time or regular basis, tend to be a premium source for ways to make the event even better the next time around.

While you are writing the survey questions, segment the survey by contact points and categories. Some of the categories for the speaker survey might include:

- Travel arrangements

- Accommodations

- Meals

- Check-in process

- Venue and space questions (location and specific room where they spoke)
- Setup of the room and venue
- Availability of staff for needs and questions

The best way to get the surveys into the hands of the speakers is to include them in the information packets they receive when they check in for the event. Before they leave from their last speaking slot, ask them to complete the survey and turn it into you. Have extra speaker survey forms on hand in case the speaker misplaces their information packet or survey form.

You also might opt to send out surveys to speakers as a follow-up to the event. With speakers, especially those who speak on a full-time or regular basis, this might not be the best way to gather the information you are asking to receive. They tend to get busy, jet off to their next speaking engagement, and never complete the survey you send to them. Some speakers will complete and return the survey to you, but asking for it after the fact with speakers tends to have a lower response rate than asking them to complete it before they leave your event.

If you do choose to send out surveys after the event, you can email the surveys using an online survey program, or you can send out hard-copy forms. If you choose to send a hard-copy format, you can increase the response rate by including a self-addressed stamped envelope for the attendee to return the survey to you.

From the staff

The third and final primary group to survey is the event staff. The event staff offers you an insider's view or behind-the-scenes view of the event. Since the staff is involved in running the event and making it happen, they offer information on what worked and did not work in the areas they were responsible for, as well as offering suggestions they might have gathered from their interaction with attendees, speakers, and other event staff.

When the staff is employees of your company, getting them to evaluate the event is relatively easy. You can have them complete the survey on their first day back in the office. You even can hold a meeting where all the event staff attends to discuss the event verbally. Because you have more direct access to an event staff that is internal to your company, you can choose a format that is conducive to your business.

If the staff members are volunteers, work for a company other than your own, or are from some other external source, then you should consider the distribution of surveys in a similar format those suggested for attendees and speakers — email or hard-copy.

Evaluate Feedback from Attendees, Speakers, and Staff

Gathering the information is simply the first step in the evaluation process. Once each pile of forms or online survey results is collected, then the compilation process begins. One of the benefits of using an online survey software program is that  these programs compile the results for you. If you use a hard-copy format, then someone has to compile the results and turn the results into a comprehensive format of the findings.

Whether you print out a report from the software program or a staff member compiles a report from the information gleaned from the surveys, the next step is to evaluate the results. You as the event host, or your entire event staff, discuss the report results in a "post-mortem" meeting. Going over the results together puts everyone on the same page, so everyone knows what went well, what was disastrous, or what could be improved. This also creates a good discussion platform for staff to provide input, suggestions, and feedback to elaborate on the results and findings from the surveys.

Measure the Successes

During the post-event evaluation, separate the findings into successes and wrongs. Successes and wrongs are highly subjective with each event. What turns out to be a success depends on what the goals for the event are from the start. To truly measure the success of your event, you should set the goals for your event during the planning stage.

To help get you started, here are some things you might wish to measure:

- Number of attendees
- Profit from ticket sales
- Satisfaction rate for each group

For example, an eco-friendly chemical conference for organization members might set its success rate on the number of attendees compared to its membership. The organization might have 1,300 members spread out across the country. It might set a conference goal at getting 33 percent of the members to attend the conference. If 450 members attend the event, then the organization has achieved its goal.

The same event could have multiple measures of success. In addition to obtaining the number of attendees the organization set as a goal, the same organization might also rate the satisfaction rate of the members who attended. One of the questions on the attendee survey might be to rate the satisfaction of the conference on a scale of one to ten. The goal of the organization might be to achieve a 95-percent satisfaction rating. If 95 percent of the attendees that complete the survey rate the conference at eight or higher, then the organization has reached its goal once again.

For a seminar where the goal is to make a profit off the ticket sales, then another success barometer is reaching the level of profit set during the planning process. For example, say a photographer offers a workshop on how to use lighting to enhance photos for amateur photographers. The fixed cost for the photographer to rent the venue, provide refreshments, and pay his or her assistant is $500 for the day. The photographer wants to make a $500 profit from the sale of the tickets, which means ticket sales need to equal $1,000 ($500 to pay for the costs of the event and $500 the photographer can put in his pocket). Assume the photographer charges $100 for the one-day workshop, per person. Paid attendees are 15 people. Total ticket sales equal $1,500 (15 people X $100 ticket price). The photographer can deem the workshop a success because he or she walks away with a $1,000 profit, which is double the original goal he or she set.

Mimicking Successes and Tweaking Wrongs for Future Events

The final steps you want to take after evaluating the event are to find ways to weave this feedback into your future events. In other words, you want to know the various aspects of the event that were a raging success. You want to know what was successful so that you can repeat these successful points in your future events. On the other hand, you also need to know what did or could have turned into a disaster at the event so that you make the changes necessary to make sure it does not happen again.

For example, a seminar for lawyers has 1,000 attendees. The check-in time starts at 8:30 a.m. on the day of the event. The first session starts at 9 a.m. You have a check-in table with two staff members that have a list of registered attendees in alphabetical order by last name. After checking in with one of the two staff members, the lawyers then have to write their name on a sticker name tag. The check-in table and the area become congested. The two lines are staggeringly long, and by the time the staff members check everyone in, the session started 15 minutes earlier, or you had to hold the start time of the session up until everyone is able to check in.

After the evaluation meeting, it is easy to see that the check-in process needs some tweaking. To make the process faster and more organized, you decide to add some staff members to the check-in the following year. You also decide to stagger the lines — separating lines by last name. The first line and staff member might be for lawyers whose last names are A-D. The next line is for E-H, etc. Additionally, you set up a separate table for the lawyers to prepare their name tags that is off to the side of the registration table. This helps move the lawyers from the registration table to the name tag table and keeps the registration area from getting congested and the lines from getting backed up.

There you have it, the post-event evaluation process of your seminar, workshop, conference, or event. You know who you need to complete event surveys, how to distribute them, and how to collect them. You now know and understand what you need to do to evaluate how successful your event was and what you might want to do differently the next time around.

Chapter Twelve

What You Need to Do if You Are Setting up an Event, Workshop, Seminar, or Conference Planning Business

Determine the Legal Structure of Your Business

Deciding which legal structure you would like to build your business under will be the backbone of your operation. The legal structure of your business will set the platform for your everyday operations, as it will influence the way you proceed with financial, tax, and legal issues — just to name a few. It even will play a part in how you name your company, as you will be adding Inc., Co., LLC, and such at the end of the name to specify what type of company you are. It will dictate what type of documents need to be filed with the different governmental agencies, and how much and what type of documentation you will need to make accessible for public scrutiny. Additionally, it will define how you actually will operate your business. To assist you in determining how you want to operate your business, a description of the different legal structures is provided as follows, along with a sample of documents that you may need to file with state and federal agencies, depending on where you live.

Business Entity Chart

Legal entity	Costs involved	Number of owners	Paperwork	Tax implications	Liability issues
Sole proprietorship	Local fees assessed for registering business; generally between $25 and $100	One	Local licenses and registrations; assumed name registration	Owner is responsible for all personal and business taxes.	Owner is personally liable for all financial and legal transactions.
Partnership	Local fees assessed for registering business; generally between $25 and $100	Two or more	Partnership agreement	Business income passes through to partners and is taxed at the individual level only.	Partners are personally liable for all financial and legal transactions, including those of the other partners.
LLC	Filing fees for articles of incorporation; generally between $100 and $800, depending on the state	One or more	Articles of organization; operating agreement	Business income passes through to owners and is taxed at the individual level only.	Owners are protected from liability; company carries all liability regarding financial and legal transactions.
Corporation	Varies with each state, can range from $100 to $500	One or more; must designate directors and officers	Articles of incorporation to be filed with state; quarterly and annual report requirements; annual meeting reports	Corporation is taxed as a legal entity; income earned from business is taxed at individual level.	Owners are protected from liability; company carries all liability regarding financial and legal transactions.

Becoming a Small Business

A small business is a company with fewer than 500 employees. You will be joining more than 27.9 million other small businesses in the United States, according to the Small Business Administration. Small companies make up 99.7 percent of *all* employer firms in the country and contribute more than 42.2 percent of the total U.S. private payroll. More than half are home-based and 73.2 percent are sole proprietors. Franchises make up 2 percent.

The SBA states that 518,500 small businesses first opened for business in 2008-2009. During the same period, 680,716 closed shop. However, two-thirds of newly opened companies remain in business after two years and about 50 percent are operating after five years. The odds are with startups. Just keep in mind that virtually every company that survives does so because the owners are working hard and care about their company.

Sole Proprietorship

Sole proprietorship is the most prevalent type of legal structure adopted by start up or small businesses, and it is the easiest to put into operation. It is a type of business owned and operated by one owner, and it is not set up as any kind of corporation. Therefore, you will have absolute control of all operations. Under a sole proprietorship, you own 100 percent of the business, its assets, and its liabilities. Some of the disadvantages are that you are wholly responsible for securing all monetary backing, and you are ultimately responsible for any legal actions against your business. However, it has some great advantages, such as being relatively inexpensive to set up, and with the exception of a couple of extra tax forms, there is no requirement to file complicated tax returns in addition to your own. Also, as a sole proprietor, you can operate under your own name or you can choose to conduct business under a fictitious name. Most business owners who start small begin their operations as sole proprietors.

General Partnership

A partnership is almost as easy to establish as a sole proprietorship, with a few exceptions. In a partnership, all profits and losses are shared among the partners. A profit is the positive gain after expenses are subtracted, while a loss occurs when a company's expenses exceed revenues. In a partnership, not all partners necessarily have equal ownership of the business. Normally, the extent of financial contributions toward the business will determine the percentage of each partner's ownership. This percentage relates to sharing the organization's revenues as well as its financial and legal liabilities. One key difference between a partnership and a sole proprietorship is that the business does not cease to exist with the death of a partner. Under such circumstances, the deceased partner's share either can be taken over by a new partner, or the partnership can be reorganized to accommodate the change. In either case, the business is able to continue without much disruption.

Although not all entrepreneurs benefit from turning their sole proprietorship businesses to partnerships, some thrive when incorporating partners into the business. In such instances, the business benefits significantly from the knowledge and expertise each partner contributes toward the overall operation of the business. As your business grows, it may be advantageous for you to come together in a partnership with someone who is knowledgeable about international trade and will be able to contribute toward the expansion of the operation. Sometimes, as a sole proprietorship grows, the needs of the company outgrow the knowledge and capabilities of the single owner, requiring the input of someone who has the knowledge and experience necessary to take the company to its next level.

When establishing a partnership, it is in the best interest of all partners involved to have an attorney develop a partnership agreement. Partnership agreements are simple legal documents that normally include information such as the name and purpose of the partnership, its legal address, how long the partnership is intended to last, and the names of the partners. It also addresses each partner's contribution, both professionally and financially, and how profits and losses will be distributed. A partnership agreement also needs to disclose how changes in the organization will be addressed, such as death of a partner, the addition of a new partner, or the selling of one partner's interest to another individual. The agreement ultimately must address how the assets and liabilities will be distributed should the partnership dissolve.

Limited Liability Company

A limited liability company (LLC), often wrongly referred to as limited liability corporation, is not quite a corporation, yet much more than a partnership. An LLC encompasses features found in the legal structure of corporations and partnerships, which allows the owners — called members in the case of an LLC — to enjoy the same liability protection of a corporation and the recordkeeping flexibility of a partnership, like not having to keep meeting minutes or records. In an LLC, the members are not personally liable for the debts incurred for and by the company, and profits can be distributed as deemed appropriate by its members. In addition, all expenses, losses, and profits of the company flow through the business to each member, who ultimately would pay either business taxes or personal taxes — and not both on the same income.

LLCs are a comparatively recent type of legal structure, with the first one being established in Wyoming in 1977. It was not until 1988, when the Internal Revenue Service ruled that the LLC business structure would be treated as a partnership for tax purposes, that other states followed by enacting their own statutes establishing the LLC form of business. These companies now are allowed in all 50 states, and although they are easier to establish than a corporation, it requires a little more legal paperwork than a sole proprietorship.

An LLC type of business organization would be most appropriate for a business that is not quite large enough to warrant assuming the expenses incurred in becoming a corporation or being responsible for the recordkeeping involved in operating as such. Yet, the extent of its operations requires a better legal and financial shelter for its members.

Regulations and procedures affecting the formation of LLCs differ from state to state, and they can be found on the Internet in your state's "Corporations" section of the secretary of state's office website. A list of the states and the corresponding section of the secretary of state's office that handles LLCs, corporations, and such is included in the *Corporations* section of this chapter. Two main documents normally are filed when establishing an LLC. One is an Operating Agreement, which addresses issues, such as the management and structure of the business, the distribution of profit and loss, the method of how members will vote, and how changes in the organizational structure will be handled. The Operating Agreement is not required by every state.

Articles of Organization, however, are required by every state, and the required form is generally available for download from your state's website. The purpose of the Articles of Organization is to establish your business legally by registering with your state. It must contain, at a minimum, the following information:

* The limited liability company's name and the address of the principal place of business

* The purpose of the LLC

* The name and address of the LLC's registered agent (the person who is authorized to physically accept delivery of legal documents for the company)

* The name of the manager or managing members of the company

* An effective date for the company and signature

For instance, Articles of Organization for an LLC filed in the state of Florida will look something like this:

ARTICLE I - Name

The name and purpose of the Limited Liability Company is:
Fictitious Name International Trading Company, LLC

Purpose: To conduct...

ARTICLE II - Address

The mailing and street address of the main office of the Limited Liability Company is:

Street Address: 1234 International Trade Drive
                             Beautiful City, FL 33003

Mailing Address: P.O. Box 1235
                             Beautiful City, FL 33003

ARTICLE III – Registered Agent, Registered Office, and Registered Agent's Signature

The name and the Florida street address of the registered agent are:

                             John Doe
                             5678 New Company Lane
                             Beautiful City, FL 33003

After being appointed the duty of registered agent and agreeing to carry out this service for the above mentioned Limited Liability Company at the location specified in this certificate, I hereby agree to take on the assignment of registered agent and will perform in this capacity. I further agree to adhere to all statutes and provisions associated with the proper and complete performance of my tasks, and I am knowledgeable with and agree to the conditions of my position as a registered agent as outlined in Chapter 608, Florida Statutes.

_____

REGISTERED AGENT'S SIGNATURE

ARTICLE IV – Manager(s) or Managing Member(s)

<u>Title</u>   <u>Name & Address</u>

"MGR" = Manager
"MGRM" = Managing Member

MGR   Jane Doe
                          234 Manager Street
                          Beautiful City, FL 33003

MGRM   Jim Unknown
                          789 Managing Member Drive
                          Beautiful City, FL 33003

ARTICLE V – Effective Date

The effective date of this Florida Limited Liability Company shall be January 1, 2013.

REQUIRED SIGNATURE:

_____

SIGNATURE OF A MEMBER OR AN AUTHORIZED REPRESENTATIVE OF A MEMBER

Corporation

Corporations are the most formal type of all the legal business structures discussed so far. A corporation is the most common form of business organization and is chartered by a state under its laws. A corporation can be established as public or private. A

public corporation, with which most of us are familiar, is owned by its shareholders (also known as stockholders) and is public because anyone can buy stocks in the company through public stock exchanges. Shareholders are owners of the corporation through the ownership of shares or stocks, which represent a financial interest in the company. Not all corporations start up as corporations, selling shares in the open market. They actually may start up as individually owned businesses that grow to the point where selling its stocks in the open market is the most financially feasible business move for the organization. However, openly trading your company's shares diminishes your control over it by spreading the decision making to stockholders or shareholders and a board of directors. Some of the most familiar household names, like the Tupperware® Corporation and The Sports Authority®, Inc., are public corporations.

A private corporation is owned and managed by a few individuals who normally are involved in the day-to-day decision making and operations of the company. If you own a relatively small business, but still wish to run it as a corporation, a private corporation legal structure would be the most beneficial form for you as a business owner because it allows you to stay closely involved in the operation and management. Even as your business grows, you can continue to operate as a private corporation. There are no rules for having to change over to a public corporation once your business reaches a certain size. The key is in the retention of your ability to closely manage and operate the corporation. For instance, some of the large companies that we are familiar with, and tend to assume are public corporations, happen to be private corporations — companies such as Domino's Pizza®, L.L. Bean®, and Mary Kay® cosmetics.

Whether private or public, a corporation is its own legal entity capable of entering into binding contracts and being held directly liable in any legal issues. Its finances are not directly tied to anyone's personal finances, and taxes are addressed completely separately from its owners. These are only some of the many advantages to operating your business in the form of a corporation. However, forming a corporation is no easy task, and not all business operations lend themselves to this type of setup. The process can be lengthy and put a strain on your budget due to all the legwork and legal paperwork involved. In addition to the startup costs, there are additional ongoing maintenance costs, as well as legal and financial reporting requirements not found in partnerships or sole proprietorships.

To establish your corporation legally, it must be registered with the state in which the business is created by filing Articles of Incorporation. Filing fees, information to be included, and its actual format vary from state to state. However, some of the information most commonly required by states is listed as follows:

- Name of the corporation
- Address of the registered office
- Purpose of the corporation
- Duration of the corporation
- Number of shares the corporation will issue
- Responsibilities of the board of directors
- Status of the shareholders, such as quantity of shares and responsibilities
- Stipulation for the dissolution of the corporation
- Names of the incorporator(s) of the organization
- Statement attesting to the accuracy of the information contained therein
- Signature line and date

For instance, Alabama's format for filing the Articles of Incorporation can be accessed through the state's Secretary of State Corporate Division website. The website contains instructions for filling out and submitting the document along with corresponding filing fees.

STATE OF ALABAMA
DOMESTIC FOR-PROFIT CORPORATION
ARTICLES OF INCORPORATION GUIDELINES

INSTRUCTIONS:

STEP 1: CONTACT THE OFFICE OF THE SECRETARY OF STATE AT (334) 242-5324 TO RESERVE A CORPORATE NAME.

STEP 2: TO INCORPORATE, FILE THE ORIGINAL, TWO COPIES OF THE ARTICLES OF INCORPORATION, AND THE CERTIFICATE OF NAME.

RESERVATION IN THE COUNTY WHERE THE CORPORATION'S REGISTERED OFFICE IS LOCATED. THE SECRETARY OF STATE'S FILING FEE IS $40. PLEASE CONTACT THE JUDGE OF PROBATE TO VERIFY FILING FEES.

PURSUANT TO THE PROVISIONS OF THE ALABAMA BUSINESS CORPORATION ACT, THE UNDERSIGNED HEREBY ADOPTS THE FOLLOWING ARTICLES OF INCORPORATION.

Article I The name of the corporation:

Article II The duration of the corporation is "perpetual" unless otherwise stated.

Article III The corporation has been organized for the following purpose(s):

Article IV The number of shares, which the corporation shall have the authority to issue, is _____.

Article V The street address (NO P.O. BOX) of the registered office:

_____

_____

and the name of the registered agent at that office: _____.

211

Article VI The name(s) and address(es) of the Director(s):

Article VII The name(s) and address(es) of the Incorporator(s):

_____

TYPE OR PRINT NAME OF INCORPORATOR

_____

SIGNATURE OF INCORPORATOR

Rev. 7/03

Any provision that is not inconsistent with the law for the regulation of the internal affairs of the corporation or for the restriction of the transfer of shares may be added.

IN WITNESS THEREOF, the undersigned incorporator executed these Articles of Incorporation on this the _____ day of _____, 20_____.

Printed Name and Business Address of Person Preparing this Document:

_____

Sometimes, finding the correct office within the state government's structure that best applies to your needs can be a challenge. The same office may have a different name in different states. In this case, the name of the office that provides services to businesses and corporations may be called Division of Corporations in one state, Business Services in another, Business Formation and Registration in another, and so forth. Therefore, to save you time and frustration while trying to establish a business, here is a shortcut so you can reach the appropriate office for filing Articles of Incorporation without having to search though the maze of governmental agencies in your state:

State	Secretary of State's Office *(specific division within)*
Alabama	Corporations Division
Alaska	Corporations, Businesses, and Professional Licensing
Arizona	Corporation Commission
Arkansas	Business / Commercial Services
California	Business Portal
Colorado	Business Center
Connecticut	Commercial Recording Division
Delaware	Division of Corporations
Florida	Division of Corporations
Georgia	Corporations Division
Hawaii	Business Registration Division
Idaho	Business Entities Division
Illinois	Business Services Department
Indiana	Corporations Division
Iowa	Business Services Division
Kansas	Business Entities
Kentucky	Corporations
Louisiana	Corporations Section
Maine	Division of Corporations
Maryland	Secretary of State
Massachusetts	Corporations Division
Michigan	Business Portal
Minnesota	Business Services
Mississippi	Business Services
Missouri	Business Portal

Montana	Business Services
Nebraska	Business Services
Nevada	Commercial Recordings Division
New Hampshire	Corporation Division
New Jersey	Business Formation and Registration
New Mexico	Corporations Bureau
New York	Division of Corporations
North Carolina	Corporate Filings
North Dakota	Business Registrations
Ohio	Business Services
Oklahoma	Business Filing Department
Oregon	Corporation Division
Pennsylvania	Corporation Bureau
Rhode Island	Corporations Division
South Carolina	Business Filings
South Dakota	Corporations
Tennessee	Division of Business Services
Texas	Corporations Section
Utah	Division of Corporations and Commercial Code
Vermont	Corporations
Virginia	Business Information Center
West Virginia	Business Organizations
Washington	Corporations
Washington, DC	Corporations Division
Wisconsin	Corporations
Wyoming	Corporations Division

S Corporation

An S corporation is a form of legal structure; under IRS regulations designed for the small businesses, S corporation means small business corporation. Until the inception of the limited liability company form of business structure, forming S corporations was the only choice available to small business owners that offered some form of limited liability protection from creditors, yet afforded them with the many benefits that a partnership provides. Operating under S corporation status results in the company's being taxed close to how a partnership or sole proprietor would be taxed, rather than being taxed like a corporation.

Operating under the S corporation legal structure, the shareholders' taxes are directly impacted by the business's profit or loss. Any profits or losses the company may experience in any one year are passed through to the shareholders, who, in turn, must report them as part of their own income tax returns. According to the IRS, shareholders must pay taxes on the profits the business realized for that year in proportion to the stock they own.

In order to organize as an S corporation and qualify as such under IRS regulations, the following requirements must be met:

- It cannot have more than 100 shareholders.

- Shareholders are required to be U.S. citizens or residents.

- All shareholders must approve operating under the S corporation legal structure.

- It must be able to meet the requirements for an S corporation the entire year.

Additionally, Form 253, "Election of Small Business Corporation," must be filed with the IRS within the first 75 days of the corporation's fiscal year.

Electing to operate under S corporation status is not effective for every business. However, it has proved to be beneficial for a number of companies through many years of operation. Because of the significant role S corporations play in the U.S. economy, The S Corporation Association of America was established in 1996 serving as a lobbying force in Washington, protecting the small and family-owned businesses from too much taxation and government mandates. Membership in the association is comprised of S corporations, both big and small, from throughout the nation. This includes companies such as CoorsTek, one of the world's leading manufacturers of industrial ceramic products, headquartered in Golden, Colorado.

Obtaining Financing for a Profitable Business

It is important that you become familiar with the various sources of financing available to provide you with the capital to operate your business successfully. Figures in a business's first operating budget are hardly ever concrete because you only are using numbers that are estimated to come close to what the actual expenses or revenue may end up being. However, it gets easier as you move forward from year to year. Each year that passes gives you a better financial history to work with, and you actually can get close to budgeting your revenues and expenses accurately. You would not be a typical entrepreneur if your vision were not larger than the depth of your pocket. It is easy to get caught up in the excitement and go beyond your financial means. This is where establishing a sound budget, and adhering to it, comes in to play. A budget is only as good as your ability to operate within it.

Financial Avenues to Take

Obtaining financing for your new business can be accomplished by requesting financing through banks, commercial lenders, finance companies, and government agencies designed to assist startup businesses and small business owners. However, before you start looking at what your options are when considering requesting a loan for your business, you first should be familiar with the types of financing available. By knowing the difference between these types of financing, you will be in a better position to make an educated decision as to what will best fit your needs.

Before you seek financial assistance

If you have all the money you need to start your business, you can skip this section for now. But eventually you may need to find outside sources of funding to purchase equipment or supply working capital, among other possibilities. The U.S. Small Business Administration suggests asking the following questions before seeking financial assistance:

- Is more capital needed, or are you able to manage current cash flow more affectively?

- How would you explain your need? Are funds necessary for expansion or as a cushion against risk?

- How fast do you require assistance? By anticipating needs rather than searching for funds under pressure, you can obtain the best terms.

- How substantial are your risks? All businesses have risks, and the intensity of risk will impact cost and available financing alternatives.

- In what stage of development is your business? It is most essential for needs to be met during transitional stages?

- What will the use of the capital be? Lenders will specify that capital be requested for extremely specific needs.

- What is the condition of your industry? Depressed, stable, or growth conditions call for varying approaches to money requirements and sources. In times of decline, prosperous businesses will obtain better funding terms.

- Is your business seasonal or cyclical? Financial requirements for seasonal businesses are normally short term.

- What is the strength of your management team? Management is the key factor considered by money sources.

More important, how do your financing requirements mesh with your business strategy? If you are without a business plan, be sure that writing one is at top of your to-do list. All capital sources will request to view your business plan outlining the startup and growth of your business.

Lending Institutions

You will have four different institutional lenders to choose from: commercial banks, credit unions, savings and loans, and commercial finances.

Commercial banks

A commercial bank is one of the most common forms of other people's money (OPM) that most people are already aware of or have actually used for a loan transaction before. Some people will tell you that bank money is OPM, while others will tell you that
bank money is really your own money. This argument starts because they see

borrowing money from a bank as borrowing against your own funds. For the purposes of this book, however, OPM is considered any money borrowed to use to support your business plan that — if you did not secure it from some outside source — you would not have otherwise.

The general thought is that commercial banking is the best place to get a business loan. One of the reasons is that commercial banks are insured by the Federal Deposit Insurance Corporation (FDIC) and typically have the largest selection in institutions with which a business owner can work. It is also generally true that you will stand your best chance of getting a business loan through a commercial bank. A commercial bank stands to gain money from a successful business and will not turn away one that they feel will offer a minimal risk with the potential of providing a maximum gain. They are in business, too, and are looking for smart deals to take part in.

Commercial banks offer a variety of services that include checking accounts, certificates of deposit (CDs), loans, and fiduciary services where they will hold something in trust for another, taking responsibility for its care for the other's benefit. They also accept pay drafts, and can issue the business letters of credit when they are needed. Beyond these traditional loan services, today's commercial banks also offer credit cards and mortgages to further boost your chances of obtaining funds and allowing you to spend those funds efficiently. The largest commercial banks are usually the better option for business. They can offer more perks — such as reduced fees, more local and national branches, and their ATM services are often free, no matter where you may find yourself in your travels.

When you are approaching a bank for the first time to ask for a loan, it is almost always better for you to start with a relatively small deal. You may think that you have found the deal that is going to make you millions, but the bank will see the chance of this coming to fruition unlikely. Think of your first deal as something that you can manage easily, be successful at, and turn around quickly. It will provide you a foundation of strength for future ventures and give you a lot more negotiating power for those larger deals.

During the preliminary portion of your OPM acquisition, it is also a good idea to take a deal to the bank as a practice exercise. This is especially good because a banker will tell you exactly what he or she needs in order to make the deal happen. There is no ultimate manual that can tell you everything about how to put together a package to present to the bank. Sometimes the best way to learn is through your initial mistakes and the gentle guidance of someone who is hopefully your bank ally. You may have to hear the word "no" several times before you actually will understand how to get to a "yes." Also, the economy and business practices are fluid, changing to keep up with current events as most recently seen with the housing bust that began in 2007.

Regardless of what is going on in the business climate, the best thing you can do is to do your research and create a plan based on what is going on in your market at the current time. There are different market types to be aware of when preparing to approach a bank for a loan: low, high, recession, and recovery. No matter which market you are in, though, banks want to see some basic guidelines met. They do not engage in risky loans simply because it is not their business model. If you or your venture looks to be a risk, they are likely to pass, regardless of the market. The following will increase your chances of securing a loan:

1. **Credit:** Banks follow a traditional pattern of loaning money: If they give you a loan, they expect to be paid back with interest, which is a fee paid on borrowed assets. They gauge your ability to pay them back by your credit history. If you have a history of paying back your debts, they will look more favorably on giving you a loan because you have a history of taking care of your financial obligations.

2. **Collateral:** If lending guidelines are tightening, you may consider offering up something of value as collateral for the loan. This is a step

to consider closely before going through with it, though. You need to ask yourself if you are ready to hand over your house or boat should the business be unable to repay the loan.

3. **Cosigning:** Depending on your credit history and any other factors a bank pulls into the equation, they only may feel confident in giving you a loan if you have someone cosign the loan.

4. **History:** If you have a history of doing business with a bank, they may feel more confident in working with you. Also, if you have a history of owning a business and can show a track record of success, they also may breathe a little easier in extending a loan to your new business venture.

The tighter the market, the tighter you may find a particular lender's guidelines to be. For example, in a recession, the reins of lending can be pulled in, with loans being issued in a trickle. It may be difficult for anyone to get a loan — even those with excellent credit. Banks have their own goals and bottom lines to protect, and their guidelines will remain fluid to protect their own interests. Lending may become so lean you may have no choice but to seek OPM from nontraditional means, which we will be covering.

You will find there are generally two views regarding relationships with commercial bank lenders: those who believe in using only one faithful bank and those who believe that you should have no less than three to five good, solid banking relationships in place.

The faithful banker plan

Institutional lenders are one of the most popular forms of traditional OPM, and they can become a strong ally to those with decent credit. The key thing that you must understand about institutional lenders is they expect your full patronage and will work their best efforts for you if you satisfy all of your traditional banking needs through one bank alone. Some banks can be like a jealous best friend; some banks do not like you stepping out with other banks, seeing what kinds of deals you could get, and borrowing money here and there from a number of different sources. If you want a strong ally on your team, pick an institutional lender that you really like and stick with them. Of course, if a really good opportunity comes along, you may want to try to work something out, but in general, your relationship with your bank is like a marriage in that it is best when it is a one-on-one relationship without any third parties stepping in as temptation. Business is business, but you want to conduct smart business with long-term benefits; you do not want to burn any bridges as you grow your venture.

Advantages	Disadvantages
• Forge a strong relationship with a financial ally who knows you well.	• Limits on the amount that one bank may be willing or able to lend • High or variable interest rates, making the cost of the loan greater • May take time to build a strong relationship • Your bank may close or be swallowed up by a larger bank, ending your carefully honed relationship and leaving you seeking a new one.

The "more the merrier" plan

Not all banks are upset about sharing their customers with other banks, and if they know anything about smart business, they probably should expect it. The major branches have their own specialties and can offer large sums of money to good clients, but sometimes, smaller banks are more likely to do a deal that the bigger banks would shy away from. It is not a bad idea to have as many options at your disposal as possible.

Advantages	Disadvantages
• It is a great source for OPM when all others methods have failed.	• You may have an interest rate that is high or variable. • There are limits on the amount that the bank will allow you to borrow. • Difficult to obtain money for those with a bad or nonexistent credit rating

Credit Unions

All credit unions are set up as not-for-profit, and because of this, they tend to offer much better deals for their customers. It is a cooperative-style financial institution, in that it has members who have partial ownership in the institution. The earnings actually are divided between its members in the form of dividends or reduced interest rates. There are always exceptions to this general set-up, but it is common for a credit union to offer higher deposit rates and lower fees. However, to get these better deals, you will have to pay a membership fee and then join the credit union by opening a savings account and "buying in" to a share of the union. Only a member is welcome to deposit or borrow money in any capacity. Credit unions traditionally have better rates and fees because they basically are nonprofit organizations with lower operating costs than commercial banks and are content with much more modest returns.

Credit unions are not all the same and most are not insured through the FDIC. However, the National Credit Union Share Insurance Fund (NCUSIF) protects all federal credit unions and many of the state-chartered credit unions. NCUSIF is administered by the National Credit Union Administration (NCUA). This is a federal agency responsible for chartering and supervising all of the federal credit unions, which are owned and controlled by their members as a co-op system. Most credit unions will offer the same services as banks, such as checking and credit cards, but do so under a different terminology. For example, where a commercial bank will use "checking account," a credit union will call it a "share draft account." Same service, different name. But not all of them will have the same services, and the ones that have more limited offerings also will not be as likely to offer the perks, such as convenient banking hours for those business owners who are working long hours. The best thing to do is look around at the different credit unions available in your area and rate their services and fees in comparison with some of your larger commercial banks.

Savings and Loans (Thrifts)

Savings and loans (thrifts) are similar to commercial banks in that they are in it for profit. While most commercial banks only can branch by acquisition, the chartered thrift has more freedom, and therefore, no limits in terms of waiting to find another bank they can acquire. It is actually cheaper for thrifts to branch out nationwide, benefiting the business owner with the lowest cost for services. However, one negative aspect of the federally chartered (savings and loan) thrift is that it is limited to 20 percent of assets in a business loan, a rule that remains in place as of the 2002 Office of Thrift Supervision regulatory bulletin.

Commercial Financing

Commercial financing is basically a term used to describe an asset-based lending system. In this system, the borrower is required to offer collateral in the form of personal or business assets, such as a home or other property; these assets then are used to secure the loan. The types of assets that you can gain financing on include outstanding accounts receivable, certificates of deposit, bonds, contracts for import/export, purchase orders, existing inventory, major equipment, franchise development, and existing demand for product or service.

It is never too late to begin fostering a positive relationship with a bank, and you can take a few steps in order to accomplish this:

1. Know your bank manager on a personal level, meaning that you are comfortable enough to invite them out to lunch or for coffee. They will be more willing to go out of their way for someone they know on a personal level than someone who has just walked in from off the street. Keep in mind that people conduct business with those they know and like.

2. Bankers are trained to recognize the signs of a snap business decision in need of quick cash. In general, they are not too keen on such requests because they know that the odds are slim that any due diligence has been done to determine the feasibility of the business idea. If you start building the relationship a few months before you need the loan and you throw out occasional hints that you may be in the market for a loan once you get your business plan solidified, it will improve your chances of acceptance greatly. The reason is that they will know that you have had time to consider your plan, and you are probably less risky than someone

who has thrown something together quickly and is looking for some fast money to fund it.

3. Instead of selling yourself to the banker, try to have the banker sell himself to you. You want the bank to be aware that not only are you presenting to them a great opportunity to work with an up-and-coming entrepreneur, but that you are looking at other banking options as well. You are serious about your business and being selective when deciding whom you think will be your best ally during your climb up the mountain of wealth and success. To aid in turning the evaluation away from you and to the bank, try asking the banker several questions during your initial meeting. Such questions might be:

    • How long have they been with the bank?

    • What types of clients has the banker assisted?

    • What is the bank's reputation in the business community?

    • What type of criteria does the bank use for loaning to businesses?

    • What is the bank's CAMEL (capital adequacy, asset quality, management, earnings, and liquidity) rating?

This CAMEL reference basically is asking the banker what their bank's safety and soundness rating is. They may hesitate to give this out, as it is rarely given out in public. Do not let that deter you in asking. It will show that you are serious about finding a strong bank to build a good relationship with more so than just obtaining some quick cash. Also, it will show you know what you are talking about because you have done your homework.

Joint Ventures

What interest should you have in a joint venture?

Sometimes one of the best ideas for accessing a source of money will be to partner with another business entity. This alliance between the two interested parties is not a merger as such because there is no actual transfer of ownership between the two parties. Instead, it is a decision to share assets, knowledge, market shares, and profits. The companies involved are allowed to keep what is theirs, but they combine resources in a common interest to create potentially more profit than what could be generated individually.

Joint ventures have two primary needs: helping the business learn new technology that will make the company function more efficiently, and enabling new markets to be opened to their product that they would not have otherwise had access to. If you are partnering with a large company that is interested in expanding in your operating area, this could mean that you have just found a great source of both OPM and other people's resources (OPR). A joint venture can be a great opportunity as long as you are able to find the right company with which to align your company.

A joint venture can create a rather large business out of a very small one. Sometimes, a small business can insert itself into a larger corporation in a market it would like to saturate. The larger business can engage in a joint venture with the smaller company and profit through its success, while the small business can become a rather large force in the market in a very short time. Small entrepreneurs need to understand that even they have things to offer that a larger company may want, such as an area of specialty, and if they can convince them of that, it will be as good as obtaining OPM from them.

One problem that can occur is that one of the companies will be afraid to share its technology with a potential competitor, while the other company is afraid to share its market area. If both businesses cannot find a measure of trust between one another, they will not be able to give each other the support they need in order to assure the success of the venture, therefore crippling its potential. Also, a joint venture can mean that while you will be gaining power and OPM within your business-marketing area, you also may lose a portion of the control you have over your business as a whole. In other words, you have to decide whether it is more important for you to own 100 percent of a $1-million-dollar company, or only 10 percent of a $100-million-dollar company.

Not all joint ventures are created equal

Both parties must share equally in order for an initial agreement to work effectively. Such a plan is accomplished with due diligence by checking the credentials of the other business. If both businesses can agree on a fair trade of services, then this is well worth the effort. If the parties cannot agree, then this only will lead to lost money and time — none of which a new business has the luxury of squandering — ultimately defeating the initial intent, which is to strengthen their position.

The key to the acquisition of a successful joint venture arrangement is to find a need that a similar business may have, and find a way that you could fill that need for them in a way that can be spelled out within a partnership agreement. Many joint ventures involve the combined efforts of two businesses targeting two different market areas. It is common for one business in the United States to want to partner with a business in, for example, Asia. This could be a piece of a market that would be very costly to get into without the combined efforts of a couple of businesses that form a joint venture to tackle it.

As good as this can look on paper, it is certainly not a fix-all for a business that is either stagnating or new and looking for an alternative market or technology. Out of 100 such joint ventures, only 40 percent of them will be successful by the end of five years. The other 60 percent would have dissolved long before that five-year period. Do your homework to find a qualified, developed company to venture with, and your chances of success will go up exponentially.

The most important part of any joint venture, besides negotiations, is the contract itself. Every joint venture you consider must have an agreement so that both parties know what is expected and the parameters of what will be involved. These are generally very standard and straightforward agreements. They are fairly easy to come by on the Internet, but in general, there are a few important aspects you will want to make sure get covered. The biggest concern is in what form payment will take. Will it be cash? Will it be part ownership of the business? Or is your business producing technology that the co-venturing partner may be able to use in return? Other aspects to consider include who is responsible for making decisions and operating the business day to day, who will be responsible for expenses, and under what terms the joint venture will dissolve.

Federal Government

Government agencies: There is magic in the SBA

The magic acronym for this section is SBA, otherwise known as the Small Business Administration, which was created in 1953. State and local government are supportive of small business ventures, as they stimulate the economy for a region because they often create jobs. For all the complaints people have against the government and taxes, they can learn to take advantage of the money they have put into the government and let it work for them. It has become a big help over the years because the government has realized that its best chance of getting a return is through the funding of small business programs.

The SBA is not the source for your loan, but rather the coordinator for the loan using a participating bank or institution. When an institution sees a business as unfit or too big of a risk, the SBA will step in and make as much as a 90 percent guarantee to the bank that the loan will be paid off by the SBA, regardless of what happens to the business. This handy guarantee makes banks friendlier to deal with, especially if you are getting used to being turned down. These loans are not handed over to just anyone, however; the entrepreneur must prove through an extensive application process that they will be able to pay off the loan and have collateral to back it up.

The SBA loan is a good option due to its favorable terms as compared to what you may find with conventional bank financing. SBA programs do not require a large down payment, whereas 20 to 30 percent is common for the conventional lending institution. The typical down payment for an SBA loan is 10 percent, and they have the ability to offer an amortized term of up to 25 years. The SBA also does not carry balloon loans that will drop a large bomb on the business once the loan has reached maturity.

Small businesses fall prey to the balloon loans because they initially are attracted to the relatively low payoff amount over the course of the loan. This can be beneficial in terms of managing the cash flow of the business. The problem is, if they do not save up for the large balloon payment at the end of the loan, they will be forced to refinance and incur the penalty of several fees on top of their balloon payment. With the typical loan amortization, the time between the initial loan and final judgment day is within five to ten years, which can be a delicate time for most new businesses.

The SBA helps keep money where it is needed — accessible and flowing in the small business — rather than the business depleting all of its own capital, which could potentially result in stifling its growth. These loans are also compatible for small businesses as well as the moderately small corporations. They offer loans starting from the low end of the spectrum up to $2 million to $5 million. This will not be sufficient for a Fortune 500 company, which works with multi-million-dollar loans; these programs were not designed for the big guns that small businesses have to sometimes compete against. However, these loans can help small businesses compete. Eight popular SBA programs are available today. To begin with, talk to your bank about applying for a loan through the SBA. Again, the SBA does not extend you a loan directly but works with lenders. You need to supply your bank lender with any paperwork they request in order to submit a loan application, such as financial statements, along with your business plan. If the bank is unable to extend you a loan, ask them to consider your loan under the SBA's guaranty program. Be familiar with the details of all eight of the SBA's programs.

Basic 7(a) Loan Program

This is SBA's primary business loan program. While its maximum allowable loan is $2 million, it is the SBA's most flexible business loan program in its terms and eligibility requirements, and is designed to accommodate a wide variety of financing needs. Most of these loans are given to serve functions such as working capital, machinery, equipment, furniture, renovation, new construction, and debt refinancing. Commercial lenders are the ones who actually make the loans and the determination for who they will loan to, but the government offers a guarantee for a percentage of the loan should the borrower default or fail to meet the terms of the loan. For this particular loan program, the government can guarantee up to 75 percent of the total loan made to the business if it exceeds $150,000 and 85 percent for loans less than $150,000.

The most attractive features of the 7(a) are its low down payment, low interest rates compared to most banks, and an extended loan maturity for as many as ten years for working capital and 25 years for fixed assets. These are great perks.

Should a business want to start an early payoff, a very small percentage of the prepayment amount will be charged as a prepayment fee. The early payoff can come in handy when a business is experiencing fast growth and needs to refinance in order to support its expansion, and the small fee required to do this may be more than worth their while.

Microloan Program

This short-term loan offers very small loans, up to $35,000 to small businesses that are starting up or growing. Funds are made available to intermediary lenders who are nonprofit and community-based, and these lenders typically require some form of collateral for the loan. The loan can be used as working capital to fund the operations, to purchase inventory, supplies, and equipment in order to do business, or furniture and fixtures for the business. Intermediaries are available in most states, the District of Columbia, and Puerto Rico. The states where there is no intermediary, including Alaska, Rhode Island, Utah, and West Virginia; Rhode Island and a section of West Virginia, currently are accessing intermediaries in neighboring states.

Prequalification Pilot Loan Program

This program allows a small business to have their loan applications analyzed and receive a potential blessing from the SBA before a lender or institution consider it. It covers loan applications in which the business owner is looking for funds up to $250,000, and its deciding factor involves aspects of the applicant's credit, experience,

reliability, and to some degree, character. This makes it unique among many of the other loans, where the applicant must have assets in order to be qualified.

The main purpose for the SBA in this particular program is to help the entrepreneur strengthen his or her loan application. This program can be helpful for an applicant who has relatively good credit and a semi-established business looking for expansion. The SBA will ask to see the applicant's past financial records, ratios, history, and personal credit. The SBA will help determine which sections of the loan request are potential red flags for the bank and then recommend the most favorable terms the applicant should expect.

Economic Opportunity Loans (EOL)

This program is for the low-income business owner who may be experiencing even more difficulty in securing financing despite having a sound business idea. As long as one business partner is considered to be living below the poverty level (determined by the federal government and adjusted annually for inflation) and owns at least half of the business, an applicant can qualify for EOL assistance. It is also an option for the small business that already been has declined by a conventional bank or institution. The best part of the EOL program is that the loans are long term and offer a flexible payback rate of 10 to 25 years, depending on the type of loan.

LowDoc Program

The LowDoc (short for low-document) Program is set up to make the application process much simpler, less time-consuming, and quicker than traditional methods. It does this by reducing the size of the application form to one page for loans under $50,000. For larger loans of $50,000 to $100,000, an applicant receives the same one-page application, along with a request for his or her past three years of income tax returns. This program is the most popular in the SBA's history.

CAPLines

A CAPLines loan is an asset-based line of credit, allowing businesses to manage their short-term needs, such as to continue payroll and purchase equipment. Typically, a business unable to qualify for other lines of credit, such as a builder or small company, will use this type of loan. The payback terms of a CAPLine are adjusted to fit the seasonality and cash flow of a business, such as a business trying to complete a large project and waiting for payment.

Grants

So far, we have been speaking about the many forms of government funding that have to be paid back. What if there was a way to dodge this aspect of borrowing money? There exists just such an excellent tool for some businesses, known as the grant. Grants exist because things need to get done, which requires people in order to carry out the work. They tend to center on projects where people want to help people, and the money is intended for a specific project or purpose. A business will need to meet the conditions mandated by the grant-giver, and then use the funds for the mandatory purpose. Grants must be applied for in which you respond to a Request for Proposal (RFP) and follow the criteria that has been issued as to what types of information is needed for the organization giving the grant to reach its decision. Proposals are reviewed, and the grant money is awarded to the winner(s).

While the federal government is not as generous with its use of grants for most small businesses, many local state governments are. About the only small businesses eligible for a grant these days are research firms in the engineering and scientific areas because these are capable of serving the needs of the country. These grants are through the Small Business Innovation Research Program, and you can find more information online (**www.sc.doe.gov/sbir**). Its motto, according to the website, says it all: "Supporting scientific excellence and technological innovation through the investment of federal research funds in critical American priorities to build a strong national economy… one small business at a time." Government entities recognized that small businesses were engaging in more innovation than bigger businesses, but the funding had been tilted in favor of those larger companies. This program helps level the field, so small businesses are able to compete and continue to innovate.

Beyond these few choice financing entities that answer the need of the federal government, the small business can find yet another ally closer to home than they may have realized: their state government. Every state has its own rules and privileges, so you will need to contact your state's economic development center. Research their website to see what they offer. A list of these websites can be found in the state resource website guide at the back of this book.

Government grants are created to fulfill specific purposes and can have very narrow qualifying requirements. You may not find a government grant that you can fulfill, nor be able to fit within its stringent guidelines. But the government is not the only entity that offers grants. In addition to government grants, there are three more types of grants: foundations, corporations, and individuals.

1) **Foundations:** An alternative to government grants is available through the private sector via foundations. About 100,000 foundations may be interested in what you do and might be willing to provide you with the cash to bring your idea to fruition. For example, if your business idea involves an eco-safe cleaning service, an eco-friendly foundation may be willing to offer you a grant. For more information on foundation grants, go to **www.foundationcenter.org**.

2) **Corporations:** Many companies set up programs in which they offer grants or will match money for the development of products and services that match their industry, and sometimes also resources such as their expertise or equipment. Typically, they offer grants to nonprofit organizations within their community to show support for local causes. If your business idea is to establish a nonprofit organization, look around your community for existing businesses that already are involved in the type of outreach programs that align with your idea.

3) **Individuals:** Generally, wealthy philanthropists set up foundations through which they issue grants. Again, it will depend on your business idea and if it strikes a chord with someone who is interested in what you are trying to accomplish, especially if your endeavor is civic-oriented. Individual grants are very competitive, and the guidelines can be very specific in what the grant provider wants done with their money. So, if you cannot find any grant opportunities through the government, foundations, or other corporate entities, an individual philanthropist could be a viable option.

Other Ways to Finance a Business

1) Giving — Contributions can serve as a primary source for business financing.

2) Borrowing — Other ways you can borrow money

3) Selling — Even though selling a part of your business to investors may bring in much needed capital, sharing this portion can cause difficulties.

4) Earning — The most effective way to promote growth is to manage money wisely and save calls for long-term planning.

5) Pledging — Depending on efforts to give back to the community, development grants will be accessible for public or private businesses.

6) Sharing — Team up with a sponsor, employer, business, or individual who will agree to fund your idea while coming closer to reaching their own ultimate goal.

Examining your business and discovering your entrepreneurial style are the first steps in finding the funding that matches your company's needs. When the need for money arises, entrepreneurs can become consumed by raising capital. Their judgment becomes clouded and their decision-making ability compromised. The cliché "the end justifies the means" is not always true. Your first step in exploring your financing options is to determine what you are willing to sacrifice.

Available financing sources

The following overview outlines the types of financing available to businesses. Making the decision to start or expand a small business opens up a variety of considerations and options. Many burgeoning companies spend far too much time chasing down funds from sources that do not mesh with their business. Making the right deal with the right investors or lenders provides you with the opportunity to grow in a manageable and hospitable environment. Making the wrong deal with the wrong investors can cause serious problems down the road, setting you up for conflicts and even potential failure.

Give it: Your personal investment

Investors and lenders will expect you to provide a significant amount of the capital necessary to launch or expand your business. When an entrepreneur puts assets on the line, it sends the message that he is committed to making the company a success, making it easier to acquire supplemental funding from outside sources.

There are a few exceptions, such as seed money programs created to assist economically disadvantaged, at-risk individuals. It is recommended that you have enough money saved to live for three years, as your business most likely will not make a profit in the first year or two.

Investing your money

Nearly 80 percent of entrepreneurs rely on personal savings to begin a new enterprise. Using personal savings secures the entrepreneur's control and ownership of the business. Because it is your money, no debt is incurred, and future profits are not shared with investors.

Converting personal assets to business use is the same as giving your business cash. Not only will you avoid purchasing these items, but you also will be able to depreciate them. Your accountant will set up the conversion and depreciation schedules. For many people, their greatest personal asset is their home.

Lines of credit, refinancing, and home equity loans often are used. Raising cash this way can be risky. Personal credit cards, signature loans, and loans against insurance policies and retirement accounts are other common ways of raising startup capital.

Home equity loans

You will need to know the equity you have in your home. For less than $500, an appraiser or real estate agent can locate home sale comparisons for you to use as an estimate.

If you own your home outright, you can refinance without staking all of the equity you have in your home, leaving room for future refinancing should something go wrong. If you own 20 percent or less in equity, by no means should you ever consider borrowing against that. The funds you gain will be minimal, and the second lender will not hesitate to foreclose should trouble arise.

The best way to determine feasibility is by following these steps:

1) Get your home appraised; if the value has gone up, you may own more equity than you think.

2) Figure out exactly how much you still owe on your mortgage.

3) Take the appraisal valuation, and subtract your debt to determine the amount of equity.

4) Figure out your percentage by dividing your equity amount by the valuation amount. If it is less than 50 percent, you should find a different source of capital for your business.

5) If your equity is more than 50 percent, you may be in business. Now is the time to get loan quotes.

6) Figure out how your business plan will be affected by this cash infusion, and make projections for how long it will take for the loan to be paid off.

Pay down the principal balance of the debt in order to get out of debt faster and regain the equity on your home.

Leveraging your credit

Leveraging your personal credit worthiness is another way to support your business. A new business has no established credit. Your signed personal guarantee will help establish credit for your business. Ask your attorney about personal liability issues for all business debts. Protecting your personal credit and financial health is a key reason to incorporate.

Borrow it: Loans to repay

Borrowing can either rescue your business or act as a burden to your company. When researching different types of loans, keep in mind such issues as collateral required, interest rates, and repayment terms.

Loans from family and friends

When searching for capital, a smart move would be to ask those who are close to you for assistance. Because you have established a relationship with your family and friends, they will not question whether to trust you, and a desire to help already will be present.

Instead of turning to the bank, friends and family can offer to help start up a business by providing interest-free or low-interest loans. This way, control is in full hands of the business owner. There may even be an angel investor in the family.

When considering these investors, ask yourself five questions:

1) Will this person panic about money after investing?

2) Does this person understand the risks and benefits?

3) Will this person want to take control or become a nuisance?

4) Would a failure ruin your relationship?

5) Does this person bring something to the table, besides cash, that can benefit my company and me?

Credit Lines

Many small businesses are drawn to microloans. These loans provide a short-term borrowing option and are typically safer because they have lower rates of interest. Microloans can help close the gap between manufacturing costs paired with delivery, and the time needed to receive full payment from customers. Credit lines help in making sure payroll is met.

Sell it: Shared ownership

Investors are a type of owner, which means you must be willing to "sell" a portion of your business and future profits. Some investors are active participants in daily operations, while others offer guidance and support through board meetings. Still, others prefer to let you do it all while they reap the rewards.

Earn it: Creative ways to earn cash

Some entrepreneurs have discovered nontraditional ways to launch or expand a business. Networking with other entrepreneurs and locally established businesses is an excellent way to find creative solutions to financing your company. Here are some creative ways other entrepreneurs have used to earn cash and discounts.

Saving

Trimming costs, taking advantage of banking discounts and rebates, and starting a business savings plan should have first priority. Make regular deposits to start your future.

Bartering

The world's oldest economic system is a great way to pay for products and services your company needs. The Web has made connecting with other interested parties easy and has introduced bartering programs in which a series of barters can be put into play to earn bartering points.

Buying groups

These groups maximize vendor/supplier discounts and reduce costs for entrepreneurs needing everything from office supplies to raw materials. Some are free, while others require a membership fee.

Rebate programs, co-op and marketing funds, support freebies

These vendor-sponsored programs can be used to reduce your inventory costs, pay for advertising expenses, train employees, improve productivity, and decrease turnaround times.

Competitive awards

Companies compete in local, state, and national "contests" for financial and support awards based on inventions, technological advances, excellent customer service, and hiring practices.

Employee ownership programs

Earn the money you need to launch a franchise. Domino's Pizza rose to the second largest pizza chain by assisting employees in owning their own franchise stores.

Materialize Your Business

Now that you have had the opportunity to familiarize yourself with the different types of legal structures in which you can establish your operation, it is time to look at the steps necessary to make your business a reality. Starting with the most basic step, set up a place from where you can start working by getting your stationery printed so you can begin operations.

Set Up a Temporary Office

A temporary office is a location from where you can conduct all the preliminary research of determining exactly what kind of business you want to establish. This preliminary work will then provide you with the information you need to select an appropriate name for your business, such as adding LLC or Inc. at the end of it. It will determine the extent of the paperwork that will be involved and give you a better idea as to what kind of location you will ultimately need to operate your business.

To do all this preliminary work, a home office works great. Start by setting aside room in your office for all the basic equipment you will need and enough room to spread out your research material. In addition, if you are establishing this operation with partners, you are going to want to have a setting available where private discussions can be held, rather than at the local coffee shop.

Items that you absolutely must have include:

- A desk with a comfortable chair
- A filing cabinet

- A printer/copier/scanner combination

- A telephone with fax and answering machine capabilities

- A laptop computer, allowing you the flexibility to take the information with you, should you need to travel as you work toward getting your business started

- Internet access

Having Internet access from day one is essential. As there are still very rural areas in the country where high speed Internet is not available through the telephone service provider or cable network, investing in a USB broadband connection device is worth the expense. These devices are available through your cellular phone service provider and are billed as if it was another cellular phone line. Another alternative is to acquire service through a satellite receiver; however, in addition to your monthly fees, there is an initial one-time setup cost, because the equipment that needs to be installed at your office can be quite costly.

If you initially are going to set up your office at home, it will be a good idea to install a separate business telephone line. It will be more professional to have your business answering machine answer when you are not available than to have a family member take a message for you. Remember that first impressions, even through telephone contact, are critical, and you will be conducting business with people from all around the world who have no idea about the extent of your operation. An answering machine will give the caller a visual impression of a professional office, whereas a family member says loud and clear "small home office," which unfortunately often is not perceived as professional.

There is nothing wrong with purchasing pre-owned office furniture and equipment, as neither usually shows much wear. Keep in mind that your purpose is to establish and operate a business that will be financially successful. Therefore, it is important to spend your startup money wisely, as you will be building your company from there.

Fictitious Name Registration

If your business name is different than your real name, most states require that you file a fictitious name registration, DBA registration, or some form of similar registration that specifies that the name you are using to conduct business is not your own. The agency with which the fictitious name or DBA name is filed varies from state to state. In some states, the registration is done with the city or county in which the company has its principal place of business. However, the majority require the registration to be done with the state's secretary of state's office. Of all 50 states, the only ones that specifically do not require any type of filing when conducting business with a name other than your personal name are: Alabama, Arizona, Kansas, Mississippi, New Mexico, and South Carolina. Washington, D.C., makes it optional, and Tennessee does not require such filing for sole proprietorships or general partnerships.

Once you have determined your perfect company name — one that means something to you, makes you stand out, and sets you apart from the competition — then you can create an image for your business. Creating an image of how you want your company to be perceived by the general public, customers, and suppliers is quite significant, as people will identify with it and relate with what your company is truly all about. Part of creating and developing your image, as your business grows, is cultivating your company's professional attitude, culture, and business ethics.

An integral part of this image is your business logo. The logo must be unique and different from anyone else's, because the last thing you want is to have your company mistaken for another. Graphic artists, marketing agencies, and print shops are excellent places to go to for the design of your logo — make sure to ask them for a high-resolution digital copy so you can reproduce it for all your business stationery and marketing needs. In addition to being able to find an abundance of graphic artists on the Internet, marketing agencies and print shops always have graphic artists as part of their staff. You also will be able to find marketing agencies and printing companies on the Internet. However, tapping into your local talent by using local professionals is always a good idea, and for that, your local phone book is the best source of information.

Obtain an Employer Identification Number (EIN)

All employers, partnerships, and corporations must have an employer identification number, also known as a federal tax identification number. You must obtain your EIN from the IRS before you conduct any business transactions or hire any employees. The IRS uses the EIN to identify the tax accounts of employers, certain sole proprietorships, corporations, and partnerships. The EIN is used on all tax forms and other licenses. To obtain one of these, fill out Form 55-4, obtainable from the IRS at **www.irs.gov/businesses/small**. *Click "Small Business Forms and Publications."* There is no charge. If you are in a hurry to get your number, you can get an EIN assigned to you by telephone, at (800) 829-4933.

Also request the following publications, or you can download them via the Internet at **www.irs.gov**:

1) Publication #15, circular "Employer's Tax Guide"

2) Several copies of Form W-4, "Employer Withholding Allowance Certificate." Each new employee must fill out one of these forms.

3) Publication 334, "Tax Guide for Small Businesses"

4) Request free copies of "All about O.S.H.A." and "O.S.H.A. Handbook for Small Businesses." Depending on the number of employees you have, you will be subject to certain regulations from this agency. Their address is: O.S.H.A., U.S. Department of Labor, Washington, D.C. 20210, **http://osha.gov**.

5) Request a free copy of "Handy Reference Guide to the Fair Labor Act." Contact: Department of Labor, Washington, D.C. 20210, **www.dol.gov**

The IRS has developed a website called the Small Business Resource Guide, which has been specifically designed to better assist the small business owner and those who are just starting up their new business venture. This guide can be accessed online at **www.hud.gov/offices/osdbu/resource/guide.cfm**. Through this website, new business owners can access and download any number of the necessary forms and publications required by the IRS.

Open a Bank Account

Establishing a strong working relationship from the very beginning with a well-established financial institution is essential in ensuring your financial success. When you are starting up a business venture, it is sound practice to seek the advice of business professionals in their fields of expertise, such as in the banking industry. Taking the time to meet with a bank representative at the time you go to open a business checking account is time well spent, and you will be surprised as to the many services available and the sound financial advice you can receive from bank officials. Discuss your plans with a representative specializing in international business, not only for starting up your business, but also where you foresee your business going in the future. This information will allow the bank representative to advise you as to what type of business checking account will best suit your needs. He or she also can provide you with information regarding services provided by the bank, which could benefit you during the early stages of your business and in the future. This is also a good time to find out about the bank's policy on a business line of credit account, which is beneficial to have when starting a new venture. A line of credit account is an arrangement through a financial institution whereby the bank extends a specified amount of unsecured credit to the borrower.

In order to establish a business checking account, most financial institutions will require a copy of the state's certificate of fictitious name filing from a partnership or sole proprietor, or an affidavit to that effect. An affidavit is a written declaration sworn to be true and made under oath before someone legally authorized to administer an oath. To open a business checking account for a corporation, most banks will require a copy of the Articles of Incorporation, an affidavit attesting to the actual existence of the company, and the EIN acquired from the IRS.

Now that you are entering into the international market, the first element you need to look for when you are in the market for a financial institution is a bank with a strong international department. A banking institution with an international department — such as Bank of America®, Wells Fargo®, and Regions Bank®, to name a few — will be able to handle and process specialized transactions, such as foreign exchange payments and letters of credit. Letters of credit are documents used by financial institutions to guarantee payments on behalf of its customers — the buyer of the goods — thereby facilitating the business transactions between two parties. In addition, you would want the bank to provide other services, such as speed in handling transactions, electronic banking, a strong but flexible credit policy, and a good solid relationship with other financial institutions overseas.

Secure an Accountant or Purchase Accounting Software

Deciding whether to secure an accountant or purchase financial software for your business accounting needs ultimately will be up to you. It all depends on the size of your operation, as well as your knowledge of accounting principles. If you feel comfortable enough to keep your accounting records, then purchasing good accounting software should suffice. However, it is recommended that you still have an accountant look over the business records at the end of the year to ensure accuracy when it comes to closing out the year and filling out tax returns. Several accounting software packages are available in the market today, but you have to be careful which one you choose. Some are very limited and only include payroll, invoicing, and general recordkeeping. One of the most widely used packages, known for its all-encompassing versatility, is QuickBooks® financial software. The basic version of this program, QuickBooks Pro, sells for approximately $249.95 at office supply retailers, and has the capability of doing everything from invoicing, keeping track of sales tax, all income and expenses, and even printing checks. QuickBooks "Premier Edition" is a complete accounting system for your business and more. You can create forecasts, a business plan, and even do your budgeting, and it sells for approximately $399.95. QuickBooks also can be purchased online directly from the QuickBooks website at **www.quickbooks.intuit.com** or other sites such as **Amazon.com**.

If your strengths are not in accounting and recordkeeping, you should secure the services of an accountant, at least during the first year of operations or until you are comfortable enough to do the company's recordkeeping yourself. Accurate recordkeeping is essential in maintaining your company's finances, and sometimes this is something that only an accountant can do accurately. Knowing exactly where you stand financially at any given time will influence a number of business decisions that must be made on short notice, and will either help or hinder your company financially.

Get a Post Office Box

Regardless of whether you started by establishing a temporary office at home or you elected to go ahead and acquire a location for your business, securing a post office box at your nearest post office is a good idea. As a convenience to its customers, the U.S. Postal Service has now made it even easier to secure a post office box by providing this service online. Enter the U.S. Postal Service website at **www.USPS.com** and look under "Products and Services." There you will find

"P.O. Boxes Online," and it will walk you step-by-step through the process of setting one up.

Having a post office box for your company helps keep your business's correspondence separate from your personal correspondence. Most important, it will prevent you from having to reprint any business stationery, should you decide to relocate your office later. Continuity in any business means stability, which is what business partners across the borders (as well as those in the United States) look for when establishing long-term business relationships.

Permits and Licenses

City business license

You almost certainly will need a city business license if you are operating within a city, and you may need a county permit if not located within city boundaries. You can find out more about what licenses and permits you may need, where to get them, and how much they will cost by calling your city hall or county clerk's office. In most cities, the city clerk does not issue business licenses, but can direct you to the correct office if you cannot find it on your own.

You need a city license for several reasons, starting with the fact that you can be fined heavily for running a business without the correct permit. You also need to show your customers that you are legitimate, and you will need a city business license in most states to get your sales tax permit.

When you contact the agency that issues the city business license, ask how long the license is good for, what the renewal process is, whether there are levels of licensing and what level you need, how much it will cost, and whether there is anything else you need to do to be "street legal" as a business within your city or county.

State sales tax permit

Anything you actually sell, such as books, products, or software, will be subject to sales tax, and you could end up with a hefty fine by not reporting and paying sales tax as required by your state.

You can contact your secretary of state's office to apply for your sales tax permit. You will need, in most states, a local business license to do this. Make sure you allow time to get your city license and sales tax permit before you open shop. Ask the agency issuing the permit whether it needs to be renewed annually, how to do that, how and where to file and pay sales taxes, and whether you need to know anything else in order to meet your obligations to the state regarding sales taxes.

In some states, it may be difficult to find information on the Internet about exactly how to apply for your sales tax permit. Calling or sending a written request for information may be the best route to obtain the information you need.

State and county permits/licenses

Depending on where you live, there may be state or county permits or licenses required to start a business. You should call your secretary of state's office (or ask when you call about the sales tax permit) and your county clerk's office, just to make sure you are not missing anything you need to apply for.

How to know you have covered it all

The best way to make sure you have everything done is to ask someone who knows you. Again, the SCORE and SBDC are good resources for this; you also may want to call your local chamber of commerce and ask whether someone can help you make sure you have covered everything for your startup licensing and permits. Talking with someone doing business in your area can be a big help in making sure that you are complying with all the relevant laws and regulations.

Conclusion

As you went through this book, thousands of workshops, seminars, and conferences were taking place around the world. You might be looking to host seminars, workshops, or conferences for traditional methods, which is for employers to send employees to learn about the industry in which they work. You might prefer to host seminars, conferences, and workshops, where companies, experts, and associations share information on the latest trends in an industry and provide valuable tips and advice on a number of topics.

Whether you read this guide because you are thinking about hosting your own seminars or workshops for your business or because you are in charge of planning and running a seminar or workshop for your company, association, or other membership group, this guide provides you with all the information you need to make it a raging success.

The Complete Guide to Running Successful Workshops & Seminars is your stepping-stone to planning and pulling off an effective conference that is sure to be a hit from start to finish. You now have read and have everything you need to plan a seminar or workshop at your fingertips.

Now that you have read the guide for the first time, take some time to absorb the information. A large amount of work and effort goes into planning any type of seminar, workshop, or conference. Because of this, this book is a comprehensive guide that contains a large amount of information. Allowing it to soak in and to start thinking of ways to put the information to good use will make your efforts even more successful when you are ready to implement the steps to planning your event.

You have the big-picture view and all the information you need to start tackling the steps. Now, it is time to go through the book a second time. This time around, stop after each section to complete the exercises or work out the details for that particular aspect of the event. In other words, it is time to create your own blueprint for the seminar, workshop, or conference that you are planning.

Glossary

A

á la carte. This is a French term, which in a direct translation means "from the menu." In the world of seminars, workshop, and conferences, á la carte options allow attendees to choose the sessions or events they attend, rather than purchasing a package. In some instances, á la carte options are available in addition to the package deal.

attendee. The individual who is registered to participate in the event. Attendees include audience members, but they also include the speakers, vendors, exhibitors, and anyone else that is involved in the workshop or seminar.

attendance. This is the overall number of attendees.

advance registration. This is when attendees are able to register to participate in the event ahead of time. Advance registration occurs via a website, email, by phone, or by fax. See also, **early-bird registration**.

agenda. A timeline of the events at the seminar or workshop. An agenda typically includes a description of the time slots and the topic, event, or session taking place during the time allotted.

AV. AV is short for audiovisual. This pertains to any audio or visual equipment required to produce the event. Examples include microphones, amplifiers, projectors, laptops, and other sound equipment.

appetizer. As opposed to a large meal, this is smaller bites of food served while attendees are standing or seated. These are also referred to as hors d'oeuvres. In some cases, this food is served before a full-course meal. Heavy appetizers might replace a full-course meal.

amenity (amenities). Extras or complimentary items, products, or services that accompany paid items. In hotels, amenities might include ice water pitchers, glasses, and writing supplies on attendee tables. Make sure that the venue contract you have lists which items you pay for and which items are complimentary.

a/v contractor/company. Business and professional that supplies the audio and visual equipment. These suppliers typically set up, operate, and take down the equipment.

Act of God. This is a term you should be familiar with when signing contracts with your vendors. An Act of God is extraordinary and natural occurrence that is out of the control of the contractor or service provider. Examples include hurricanes, floods, tornadoes, and earthquakes. Because the occurrence is out of the control of the contract, it makes it impossible for them render the service or provide the product per the contract. Therefore, it eliminates the legal responsibility of the parties when one of these events occurs.

B

badge. Name tag or identification tag seminar, workshop, and conference attendees wear. It identifies participants as an attendee of the event and can be used for access to various areas of the venue and the event.

breakout sessions. Small group sessions that run simultaneously. Each breakout session tends to focus on a specific niche or topic. The small group environment fosters learning and interaction.

break. Short time period in between sessions or activities so participants can use the restroom, grab refreshments, make phone calls or check email.

business center. An office-type environment with office equipment, such as computers, printers, copy machines, and fax machines available for attendees to use.

business attire. Business suits or jackets with shirts and ties for men and day dresses or suits for women; usually taken to mean office and not recreational wear. Can include informal forms of national dress.

business casual attire. Dress slacks or khakis and a polo or button-down shirt. Suits, ties, and pantyhose are not required for business causal attire.

banquet setup. Seating arrangement where round tables are used, similar to a restaurant style, so that it facilitates the serving of food.

boardroom setup. Seating arrangement where rectangular or round tables are set with chairs on all sides to facilitate discussions.

C

caterer. A professional company that supplies food and beverages for your event. Generally, this is a third-party food provider that is separate from the venue. Some venues, however, do not permit outside caterers, so you have to use their onsite food and beverage department instead.

catering. Food and beverages.

check-in. The process attendees go through to let the event host know they have arrived. It is also the time attendees pick up their registration packets of information. If an attendee did not preregister for the event, they can do so during the check-in process.

check-in time. The period of time when the registration desk or table opens and starts processing attendee check-ins.

classroom-style setup. Rectangular tables facing the speaking with chairs on one side of the table, so that those seated are also facing the speaker. Classroom style also might be just chairs set up in rows, similar to assembly style, where attendees sit facing the speaker.

continental breakfast. Breakfast foods, such as cereal, pastries, fruit, juices, hot tea, and coffee.

corkage fee. If you are serving alcohol during any portion of the event, the venue charges this fee for opening each bottle when you bring your own bottles onto the premises.

contract. Legal agreement you as the event host enter into with each of your service providers that are providing the event with products and services. This agreement spells out the details of the agreement, compensation amount, and is signed and dated by the parties that are entering into the agreement.

centerpiece. Decorative item for the center of a table.

cancellation clause. Terms and conditions that allow one party of the legal agreement to cancel the product or service offering of the other party of the contract.

cash bar. This type of bar requires the guests or attendees to pay for each of their own alcoholic beverages at an event.

confirmation. Verification you receive from a vendor after entering into an agreement with them to contract their products or services. As the event host, you also might send a verification notice to attendees to confirm their registration for the event.

compensation. Payment for the receipt of products or services.

canapés. Another term for hot or cold appetizers or hors d'oeuvres.

catering room/kitchen. A room or area used for preparing the food and beverages for serving in the main event room. A staging area where the prepared food is brought on site before serving.

commission. A payment made for referring a buyer to a business.

complimentary. A product or service that is free of charge. Typically, these free items come along as part of paying for another product or service.

complimentary room. A room provided free of charge. Generally, the room comes free of charge because you have paid to book another area of the venue.

concierge. An individual that works for the venue where the event is being hosted. They are responsible for helping the event host and attendees with entertainment options, booking travel, restaurant information, and other information on the hotel and the immediate area where the event is.

charter. Renting private transportation for the use of your event attendees. Examples include a private jet, boat, or bus.

conference center. A venue with the sole purpose of providing space for meetings, conferences, workshops, and seminars.

conference pack/kit. Information package that contains forms, documents, handouts, and other information attendees need for the workshop, seminar, or conference they are attending. The kit tends to be presented in a folder, binder, or bag to make it easier for attendees to carry and use.

classroom setup. Rectangular tables arranged in rows facing the stage with seating positioned behind each table so attendees are facing the speaker. It is similar to a standard classroom layout in a school classroom.

D

deposit. Amount of money paid to hold a room or venue, or book a product or service provider. Generally, it is a percentage of the total amount of the products or services you are buying for the event.

destination management company (DMC). An event planning company that specializes in planning workshops, conferences, and seminars for clients that are in another city. The DMC is a company local to where you are hosting the event, so they have the local contacts necessary for any product or service you might need for the event. They charge a fee for their planning services.

dance floor. Platform put down in the room so that attendees can dance. Some venues have their own dance floor available for rent. Other times, you might have to rent one from a party supply company.

dress code. The preferred type of clothing for attendees, staff, and speakers to wear during the event. Business, business casual, and casual are a few examples of dressing styles.

departure time. Time to leave the venue.

database. A collection of contact information on all prospective attendees, vendors, exhibitors, and registrants. Also might be referred to as a mailing list or contact list.

E

exclusive use. When you book the use of a venue or space, this type of use provides you with private use for you and your attendees, where the outside public or other event attendees will not be allowed.

entertainment. Activity, performance, or show with the purpose of entertaining or amusing attendees.

event. A planned occasion with a specific purpose. An event can be of a social nature or more of a business purpose, including meetings, conventions, exhibitions, conferences, special events, galas, and more

exhibition. For short, it is also known as an exhibit. An event product or service providers have an opportunity to showcase their wares.

exhibition floor (exhibit floor). The area of a conference designated for exhibit space. It is usually separate from the other areas of the conference or events, such as speaking rooms, breakout-session rooms, etc.

exhibition plan (exhibit plan). The diagram of the layout of the exhibition space, including tables, booth space, chairs, and any other items required by the vendors to display their products and services to attendees.

exhibitor. A business, individual, or organization showcasing its products or services at an exhibition.

early-bird registration. Registration period for an event, workshop, conference, or seminar where registrants can register for a reduced fee. It is an incentive for attendees to register early, so the host has money up front with which to use for paying for the event itself.

exhibit booth/stand. Specifically measured area of exhibition plan for individual or organization to showcase their products and services. Its size depends on the number of exhibitors and the room capacity. Can be space only or constructed shell-schemes. Exhibitors often pay to use this space.

F

floor plan. The schematics or blueprint of a room that shows the layout. Event hosts use the floor plan to create the layout of the room and overall flow of the event traffic.

food & beverage. The catering department of a venue, such as a hotel or resort. Food & Beverage is the onsite catering department.

feedback. The evaluation process where attendees, speakers, staff, and other event participants provide thoughts, suggestions, and observations the event host can use to improve future events.

full onsite event management. A third-party company plans and implements the entire event on behalf of the event host. This type of management includes the event professionals being at the venue throughout the entire event from setup to breakdown in order to keep the event moving along according to the agenda.

first option. A right provided to the event host by the venue to accept or refuse the use of a specific space before booking. Typically, this comes into play when another client of the venue wants to use the space. The venue will contact the original client to see if they want to book this space before them allowing the other party to book it. In other words, it gives you the first right of refusal.

G

group arrivals/departures. Document that lists the arrival and departure schedule of the event attendees. Generally, this information is provided to the check-in desk of the hotel where group bookings are so that the hotel desk is properly staffed. The same list is also useful for the event staff to greet attendees or hand out information to them upon arrival. For departures, the information is useful for the front desk for checkout purposes. It is also useful to the event staff to help coordinate airport shuttles or other transportation services in bulk.

group booking. Volume reservations rather than individual ones. Generally, group booking brings a reduced rate per person to the event host than if each individual attendee books his or her own accommodations or other service.

group rate. This a prenegotiated fee specifically for the attendees and those individuals that are somehow associated with the event. The rate could apply to hotel room rates, excursion rates, travel costs, transportation expenses, and more.

H

handout. Information provided to attendees as a supplement to the information speakers share at the event. It is typically a hard-copy form of the speaker's presentation or information that complements the presentation.

I

invoice. An itemized bill of the products and/or services a vendor provides for the event.

in-house. Products or services provided on site and within the venue location.

K

keynote. The headliner or opening speech at an event. This inaugural event tends to set the tone and theme for the rest of the event.

keynote address. This is the headliner for the event; the first speech or discussion that kicks off the start of the event.

keynote speaker. The speaker that delivers the headliner that kicks off the event. This speaker is generally a professional in the field, a motivational speaker, a public figure, or celebrity.

L

laser pointer. A small device that emits a light out. Speakers, lecturers, and presenters use it to point out items and highlight special points during their presentation.

LCD. Stands for liquid crystal display. This is a type of television screen or computer monitor used to display presentations, DVDs, and other information during presentations.

LCD projector. Device used to project presentations for an event, conference, seminar, or workshop onto a LCD screen.

lead time. The amount of time the host of an event, conference, workshop, or seminar has from the time when the event is hatched until the start of the event.

lectern. A table or podium placed at the front of a room where the speaker can place his or her notes, visuals, and other information.

lobby. The entrance area of a venue. It is typically a public location that attendees of the event and other guests of the venue have access to and congregate. With conferences, seminars, and workshops, this area is often where the information and registration table is located.

M

master of ceremonies (MC). A person, usually with a microphone, that guides attendees through the event by making announcements and directing attendees, introducing speakers, etc.

motivational speaker. Professional speaker that introduces topics and speaks in a manner that uplifts the audience and motivates them in some way.

maximum capacity. The total number of people that a room or area hold.

minimum guaranteed numbers. The lowest number of attendees you will pay for when it comes to food and beverages, which is a level that is written into the contract with the food and beverage provider or catering company.

N

networking. An opportunity to interact and exchange information with prospective clients and/or referral sources.

nonrefundable. Term or condition when the payment you have made for a service or product is lost, even if you do not use the product or service, or cancel the product or service.

nontransferable. Term or condition of an agreement, such as an airline ticket, or admission ticket, that is in one person's name and cannot be assumed by another named party. If the named party does not use the ticket, then the ticket is lost to them and is not usable by anyone else.

no-show. Someone who has a reservation but does not use it.

O

on consumption. Charge or fee term where the host of the event only pays for items that are used. Generally, this is a term for alcoholic beverages, so the event host only pays for the alcohol bottles that are opened, or for the individual drinks attendees imbibe.

onsite event manager. When a venue has a professional that works at the venue to help establish, plan, and implement the event.

P

podium. Platform or stage where a speaker is raised above the audience to allow for easy viewing no matter where attendees are sitting.

preregistration. Booking or reservation period before the day of the event. With seminars, conferences, and workshops, attendees can reserve their spots at the event online, by phone, fax, or mail. In some cases, event hosts offer a reduced rate for booking ahead rather than paying at the door.

proposal. A detail of services, products, and the costs associated with these products and services. Generally, it is in response to a request for the itemized information to plan the event.

Q

Q&A. Stands for questions and answers. This is the time during a presentation or speech where audience members can ask questions and the speaker answers the questions.

questionnaire. A survey tool for gathering information by having responders answer a series of questions.

R

registration area. Place where attendees can register or sign up for the event.

registration fee. The fee charged attendees to sign up for and attend the event.

registration form. The document the attendee completes so that the event host has their contact and payment information for the event.

registration pack. Information sent to registered attendees. The information provides attendees with dates, times, travel information, and any other information they need to make it to and participate in the event.

room setup. The layout or floor plan on each room in use at the event. It describes where each item, equipment, machine, or furniture should be placed and arranged.

room turnover. The amount of time it takes to tear down the existing setup of a room and arrange the new setup.

U

U-shape layout. Arrangement of a meeting room so that the tables and chairs create a U or horseshoe shape.

V

venue. A place or location where the event, conference, workshop, or seminar is taking place.

W

Workshop. Generally, this is an event with an interactive segment, so a lecture or training session takes place, and then some time is allocated for attendees to implement what they have learned in some sort of an exercise.

Appendix

Appendix A: Speaking Bureaus & Organizations

Many speaking bureaus and organizations exist to help match speakers with events that need speakers, and vice versa. Many of these organizations categorize speakers by their specialty so you can easily identify speakers that might fit your needs.

American Speakers Bureau®
(407) 826-4248
www.speakersbureau.com

Speakers Association of Hawaii
(808) 262-6533
www.hawaiispeakers.org/

International Association of Speakers Bureau (IASB)
(480) 839-1423
www.igab.org

Keynote Resource
(800) 420-4155
www.keynoteresource.com

Keynote Speakers Inc.
(650) 325-8711
www.keynotespeakers.com

Midwest Speakers Bureau
(515) 974-8305
www.speakernow.com

National Speakers Bureau
(800) 323-9442
www.nationalspeakers.com

Nationwide Speakers Bureau
(310) 273-8807
nationwidespeakers.wordpress.com

Speaker Services: Speakers, Authors
and Entertainers for Free and Fee
(310) 822-4922
www.speakerservices.com

World Class Speakers and Entertainers
(818) 991-5400
www.wcspeakers.com

Appendix B: Sample Attendee Survey

Tell Us How We Did!

Please tell us about your experience at this year's event. While we hope we did everything to your satisfaction, we know there are always areas where we can improve. Since this is your event, we want you to get out of it what came for, so please complete the survey and submit it to the information table before leaving.

Which best describes you?

Never attended event before [ ]   Attended two years ago [ ]

Attended last year [ ]   Attended three years ago [ ]

What is the likelihood you will attend the next event?

Definitely will return [ ]   Probably will not return [ ]

Probably will return [ ]   Definitely will not return [ ]

Might or might not return [ ]   Don't Know/No Opinion [ ]

On a scale from 1 to 10, where 1 is very dissatisfied and 10 is very satisfied, please rate your satisfaction with the event overall.

| 1 | 2 | 3 | 4 | 5 | 6 | 7 | 8 | 9 | 10 |

What was your favorite part of the overall event?

What was your least favorite part of the overall event?

Please rate each of the following items on a scale of 1 to 10, where 1 is very dissatisfied and 10 is very satisfied.

Parking

1	2	3	4	5	6	7	8	9	10

Wait Times

1	2	3	4	5	6	7	8	9	10

Food

1	2	3	4	5	6	7	8	9	10

Entertainment

1	2	3	4	5	6	7	8	9	10

Restrooms

1	2	3	4	5	6	7	8	9	10

Please rate the individual speaker for each session you attended.

Speaker Name:

How would you rate the overall quality of the content and information the speaker shared with you? On a scale of 1 to 10, where 1 is bad and 10 is great.

1	2	3	4	5	6	7	8	9	10

What did you like best about the speaker?

What did you like least about the speaker?

Speaker Name:

How would you rate the overall quality of the content and information the speaker shared with you? On a scale of 1 to 10, where 1 is bad and 10 is great.

| 1 | 2 | 3 | 4 | 5 | 6 | 7 | 8 | 9 | 10 |

What did you like best about the speaker?

What did you like least about the speaker?

Speaker Name:

How would you rate the overall quality of the content and information the speaker shared with you? On a scale of 1 to 10, where 1 is bad and 10 is great.

| 1 | 2 | 3 | 4 | 5 | 6 | 7 | 8 | 9 | 10 |

What did you like best about the speaker?

What did you like least about the speaker?

What topics would you like to see available sessions on at the next event?

Appendix C: Sample Speaker Survey

Tell Us How We Did!

Please tell us about your experience as a speaker at this year's event. While we hope we did everything to your satisfaction, we know there are always areas where we can improve. Since you most likely speak at other events, we also would like to learn from your experience. Please complete the survey and submit it to the information table before leaving.

Which best describes you?

Never spoke at the event before this year [ ]

Spoke two years ago [ ]

Spoke three years ago [ ]

Spoke last year [ ]

What is the likelihood you will speak again at an upcoming event?

Definitely will [ ]

Probably will not [ ]

Probably will [ ]

Definitely will not [ ]

Might or might not [ ]

Don't Know/No Opinion [ ]

On a scale from 1 to 10, where 1 is very dissatisfied and 10 is very satisfied, please rate your satisfaction with the event overall.

| 1 | 2 | 3 | 4 | 5 | 6 | 7 | 8 | 9 | 10 |

What was your favorite part of the overall event?

What was your least favorite part of the overall event?

Please rate each of the following items on a scale of 1 to 10, where 1 is very dissatisfied and 10 is very satisfied.

Travel arrangements

| 1 | 2 | 3 | 4 | 5 | 6 | 7 | 8 | 9 | 10 |

Accommodations

| 1 | 2 | 3 | 4 | 5 | 6 | 7 | 8 | 9 | 10 |

Check-in

| 1 | 2 | 3 | 4 | 5 | 6 | 7 | 8 | 9 | 10 |

Food

| 1 | 2 | 3 | 4 | 5 | 6 | 7 | 8 | 9 | 10 |

Event staff

| 1 | 2 | 3 | 4 | 5 | 6 | 7 | 8 | 9 | 10 |

Event room

| 1 | 2 | 3 | 4 | 5 | 6 | 7 | 8 | 9 | 10 |

Audiovisual

| 1 | 2 | 3 | 4 | 5 | 6 | 7 | 8 | 9 | 10 |

Equipment

| 1 | 2 | 3 | 4 | 5 | 6 | 7 | 8 | 9 | 10 |

What did you like best about the event?

What did you like least about the event?

Are there any future topics would you like to cover at the next event?

Appendix D: Sample Staff Survey

Tell Us How We Did!

As a staff person at the event, you have an insider's and behind-the-scenes view that is valuable. Please tell us about your experience at this year's event. Please complete the survey and submit it to the information table before leaving.

Which best describes you?	
Never staffed event before [ ]	Staffed two years ago [ ]
Staffed last year [ ]	Staffed three years ago [ ]

What is the likelihood you will staff the next event?	
Definitely will [ ]	Probably will not [ ]
Probably will [ ]	Definitely will [ ]
Might or might not [ ]	Don't Know/No Opinion [ ]

On a scale from 1 to 10, where 1 is very dissatisfied and 10 is very satisfied, please rate your satisfaction with the event overall.

1	2	3	4	5	6	7	8	9	10

What was your favorite part of the overall event?

What was your least favorite part of the overall event?

Please rate each of the following items on a scale of 1 to 10, where 1 is very dissatisfied and 10 is very satisfied.

Parking

| 1 | 2 | 3 | 4 | 5 | 6 | 7 | 8 | 9 | 10 |

Wait Times

| 1 | 2 | 3 | 4 | 5 | 6 | 7 | 8 | 9 | 10 |

Food

| 1 | 2 | 3 | 4 | 5 | 6 | 7 | 8 | 9 | 10 |

Entertainment

| 1 | 2 | 3 | 4 | 5 | 6 | 7 | 8 | 9 | 10 |

Restrooms

| 1 | 2 | 3 | 4 | 5 | 6 | 7 | 8 | 9 | 10 |

Venue

| 1 | 2 | 3 | 4 | 5 | 6 | 7 | 8 | 9 | 10 |

What was the biggest complaint you received from an attendee or speaker during the event?

What was the biggest compliment you received from an attendee or speaker during the event?

Do you have any suggestions on how we could improve upon the event to make it a more pleasurable experience for attendees and speakers?

Appendix E: Sample Registration Information

When & Where

- February 1: Miami, FL
- February 2: Beverly Hills, CA
- February 3: Phoenix, AZ
- February 4: Seattle, WA
- February 5: New York City, NY
- February 6: Washington, DC

Who Should Attend

Small business and entrepreneurs who have an open mind and are ready to make a change in their business.

Who Should Not Attend

Small business owners and entrepreneurs who are content with the way things are and do not see a need to make any changes. THIS SEMINAR IS NOT FOR YOU!

How

When it comes to registering for the event, you have several different options.

- Register online at www.xyzsamplevent.com
- Complete the registration form and mail it to the address on the form
- Complete and fax the form
- Register by phone (800) 555.5555

Fees

- Early-Bird Special: Register by January 2 for any of the scheduled events for only **$197** per person, per events. This is an automatic savings of **$100**.

- Preregistration from January 3 up until the day before the event is **$297** per person, per event. An additional guest from the same company is **$197** per person, per event.
- Registration at the door is **$347** per person, per event.
- Registration fees include access to all of the informational sessions, handouts, materials, and lunch.

Payment Methods

- Preregistration: Visa, MasterCard, American Express, and business and personal checks.
- At the door: Cash, Visa, MasterCard, and American Express only. NO CHECKS.

Cancellation Policy

Registered attendees can cancel up until 48 hours before the start date of the event for which they are registered. Upon cancellation, the fees will be returned to you in the same form of payment you made.

If you cancel within 48 hours of the date of the event, the fees will be a credit on file for one of our future events or on the purchase of one of products or service packages. You have up to one year from the cancellation date to use the credit.

Guarantee

If for any reason you do not feel as if the seminar material is helpful and useful for you, simply turn in all of the materials to us by the first break of the first day of the event. We will issue you a 100-percent money-back guarantee. No questions. No hassles. No problems. When the event is over, the guarantee continues. If you do not make an additional $4,000 in the year following the event from implementing the ideas and suggestions we share, let us know, and we will refund all of your money for the cost of the seminar. In all of the time we have been hosting these seminars, we have NEVER had to refund an attendees' money, but it is a guarantee that we stand behind.

Not Able to Attend?

For those that want to benefit from the information, but cannot make an in-person appearance at any of our events should contact us. We offer a home study course that guides you through the information and how to implement it to benefit your own business. Call us at (800) 555.5555 for more information.

Ready to register? Great! Use the form on the following page, register online or give us a call now. Seats are limited, so save your spot today!

Sample Registration Form

4 Easy Ways to Register:

- Online at www.xyzsamplevent.com

- Complete the registration form and mail it

- Complete and fax the form

- Register by phone (800) 555.5555

Mailing Address:

Seminars 'R Us
1234 XYZ St.
Anytown, MI USA 55555

Please choose the date and location of the event:

_____ February 1: Miami, FL

_____ February 2: Beverly Hills, CA

_____ February 3: Phoenix, AZ

_____ February 4: Seattle, WA

_____ February 5: New York City, NY

_____ February 6: Washington, DC

Name:		
Business Name:		
Address:		
City:	State:	Zip Code:
Phone:	Fax:	
Email:		

Additional Attendee Name:		
Address:		
City:	State:	Zip Code:
Phone:	Fax:	
Email:		

Additional Attendee Name:		
Address:		
City:	State:	Zip Code:
Phone:	Fax:	
Email:		

Additional Attendee Name:		
Address:		
City:	State:	Zip Code:
Phone:	Fax:	
Email:		

____ Yes, register me for the above referenced event. I am ready and willing to learn how to take my business to the next level!

____ No, I am unable to attend an event in person, but I am interested in the home study course.

Fees:

____ Early Bird (before January 2) $197 per person, per event

____ Preregistration (after January 2) $297 per person, per event

____ # of additional attendees x $197

____ Total

Payment Information

____ Check enclosed (Make payable to Seminars 'R Us)

____ Please charge my credit card

    ___Visa   ___ MasterCard   ___ American Express

    Card Number: _____

    Expiration Date: _____ 3 or 4 Digit Security Code: _____

Signature: _____

Date: _____

Bibliography

Berkun, Scott. *Confessions of a Public Speaker*. 2010

Burchard, Brendon. *The Millionaire Messenger*. New York, 2011.

Chan, Janis. *Delivering Training Workshops*. California, 2010.

Gleeck, Fred. *Marketing and Promoting your own Seminars and Workshops*. 2001.

Jolles, Robert L. *How to Run Seminars & Workshops*. New Jersey, 2005.

Karasik, Paul. *How to Make it Big in the Seminar Business*. 2nd ed. 2005.

Weiss, Alan. *Money Talks: How to Make a Million as a Public Speaker*. 1998.

Author Biography

Copywriter and marketing consultant Kristie Lorette is passionate about helping entrepreneurs and businesses create copy and marketing pieces that sizzle, motivate, and sell. It is through her more than 14 years of experience working in various roles of marketing, including running an event planning service of her own for four years, that Lorette developed her widespread expertise in advanced business, marketing strategies, and communications. Lorette earned her B.S. in  marketing and B.S. in multinational business from Florida State University and her M.B.A. from Nova Southeastern University.

Index